The 38 Days of Christmas Devotional

Let the Journey Begin

Allan Rodney Tilley

Printed in the United States of America

First Printing 2018

ISBN 9781731536877

Cover Design: Kindle Direct Publishing

Publisher: Kindle Direct Publishing

Author Contact:

Allan Rodney Tilley

1396 Hwy. 62 West

Berryville, Arkansas 72616 U.S.A.

Email: randjtilley@yahoo.com

Merry Christmas
&
Happy New Year

A Gift for You

Dedication

This book is dedicated to my good friend and former pastor, Rev. William Gage, of Philadelphia, Pennsylvania, who was a co-worker in the Lord's House, a scholar, and a man who taught me how to love the inner city of America. May you rest in peace in your heavenly home with God the Father.

Introduction

You may ask the question from the title, "Why 38 Days of Christmas?" I am sure you thought it should be the 12 days of Christmas from the songs and stories told and sung, or you may have thought that even with the addition of the Advent season we still would have only a month of Christmas, but in reality; not so. For Christmas really takes us out of one year and into the next, for you find that in the Western tradition we celebrate Christmas as the end of the year, however in the Eastern traditions of the church, Christmas is the beginning of a New Year. The Christmas dates of December 25 in the West and January 7 in the Eastern Church calendar actually make more sense for then Christ's birth is both the ending of all and the beginning of everything. He is the "Alpha and Omega," the beginning and the end, and he asks us to join him for both celebrations. Therefore, join with me and with all Christians this holiday season for "38" days of Christmas. It is a journey, a pilgrimage of the old and the new, with some starts and some finishes, with a little walking and some running, so that with eager hearts and an open spirit we can discover all that God has for us in the "38" days of Christmas. We are on a road that leads to Bethlehem, a journey, and as we walk along the way we will find that there is "Peace on earth, Goodwill to men."

Table of Contents

Day One
"The Journey Begins"

As we begin this journey on our 38 days of Christmas, I want to remind you that it may take a while to get to our final destination, and it may even take us more than the 38 days. We know that it took Jesus an eon of time to start this journey to come and take on the nature of man to reach us, all of us, with the truth of his love. Of course, it took Mary at least nine months to experience the birth of Christ on that first Christmas Day, and when you add in the Wisemen who started their journey from afar and after years of traveling, finally found the Christ-child, you come to understand that finding Christ and understanding the Christmas story is a journey of epic proportions. I do not know with which personality you identify with in the Christmas story, but I know that my journey and your journey is just starting, so let's begin and see where the journey leads.

In the past, at a church that I pastored, I had a congregation that truly identified with the Wise Men, in fact, they knew that they were the Wise Men and Wise Women, the "Social Elite" of the community. They were the wise, the educated, the upstanding citizens of the neighborhood, but in truth, that very fact, kept them from reaching out to the neighbors who lived among them. They loved the Christmas saying, "Wise Men still follow Christ," and they were sure they were the wise ones. But wait before you jump to conclusions.

The Magi,[1] the Wise Men, as we have come to understand, did not arrive on Christmas Day at all, but they came during what we now call, Epiphany. In fact, they most likely came when Jesus was a toddler, in his "terrible twos." These men from the East had followed the star and as rich learned urban men they too found the Christ-child. However, they arrived just a little too late for Christmas. When they finally did arrive, they also bowed down and worshiped the Christ, and gave gifts of lavish expense with the utmost of joy, and it was a glorious day to remember. It was an occasion of huge enlightenment when they finally figured it out and with their much study and knowledge, they had come to the place of significance of which they had sought. But they were late, none the less.

But I hate to break the news to you, some unlearned shepherds beat the Wise Men in finding Christ by years. These shepherds in the hills surrounding Bethlehem were just plain people, ordinary men, the working class, the poor, and these men, with a few mindless sheep, worshipped Christ first. The Bible says, "When the angels had left them and gone into heaven, the shepherds said to one another, "Let's go to Bethlehem and see this thing that has happened, which the Lord has told us about. So they hurried off and found Mary and Joseph, and the baby lying in the manger. When they had seen him, they spread the word concerning what had been told them about this child, and all who heard it were amazed

---

[1] Magi, Kings of the East, and Wise Men are all representations of those who visited Christ from the East in Matthew 2.

at what the shepherds said to them." (Luke 2:15-18). In fact, for the first time in their life, the lowly shepherds were finally on time for something and it was for that first Christmas day.

However, like the Magi or Wise Men, we too could study the stars and get there late, basking in our wisdom and knowledge, delighted that we and our camels had made the journey to the end, or we could be like the shepherds and arrive on time, the exact time, and then with great joy, tell what we have seen and was told. For you see, none of us are wise, except in our own eyes, but even if we were, we must understand that it was the Wise Men who followed, but it is shepherds who led. So next time when you are endeavoring to buy a Christmas bumper sticker, don't get the one that says, "Wise Men still follow Him," instead get the one that reads, "Shepherds get there first," or "Shepherds always lead." And all the sheep ranchers of Wyoming said, "Yes, and Amen."

So, join me now on these "38" days of Christmas as we make sure we all arrive, whether late or on time, for in the end the joy will be in the finding, and the finding will be "just on time."

The Christmas Story in Scripture

And it came to pass that in those days, that there went out a degree from Caesar Augustus, that all the world should be taxed.

Luke 2:1 (KJV)

Day Two
"I Found Him"

Yesterday, on "Day One" we saw that the shepherds found Christ and the Magi found him too, albeit a little late, but today as we continue our journey of discovery, you too may look for him and find him.

I have lived and served in many countries and in many churches, and under various denominations throughout the world, each having their own traditions, and each with a rich heritage of Christmas spirit. One church that I had the opportunity to be in had an interesting tradition that I thought was really innovative. They had a tiny ceramic Jesus which had been in the Christmas nativity set for years. Each year, starting with the beginning of Advent, the ceramic Jesus was placed, or should I say, hidden, in some crevice or corner of the church. Each week, when the children would arrive for church, the first order of service was to find, "Baby Jesus." With joy and excitement, the children, both young and old, would scurry all over the church, until one would yell out, "I've found him! I've found him!" And if you were the one who discovered Baby Jesus that week, you had the privilege of placing Jesus in the manger. It was a simple task, but one that the children looked forward to each week.

Every week you knew that with just a little effort, even the smallest child would be able to find Jesus. He was not really hidden, for he was strategically placed so that the children could always find the tiny ceramic Christ. There were other decorations in the church: wreaths, bows, candles, and greenery, but nothing took the place of the Christ-child.

But sad to say, I have served in other churches where there were many decorations of the "carnal type." I found things that made me want to cry and sometimes laugh. There was a time when a parishioner wanted to have a nativity set where the Wise Men were German Shepherds, Mary a Collie, and Jesus was a Beagle pup, all surrounded by a few cows and even a couple of cats as well, for as the parishioner said, "Cats are people too."

You see, at that church, Jesus was not hidden; he was not there. There were special "Christmas" programs with Christmas dinners, Christmas brunch, Christmas shopping, and people who came throughout the Christmas season, singing songs, eating sweets, and making merriment, but there was an absence of that tiny baby, the baby Jesus, who was to become the "Savior of the World." The children looked, and the adults helped, but Jesus was not there, no one could find him. Years ago, Christ had left, and no one even noticed, no one even knew.

Therefore, I ask of you, plead with you, this year, go and find the Christ-child and bring him back to the church, back to your home, back to your heart. Make it easy and please do not hide Him, so that the young and the old, the rich and the poor, are able to exclaim with joy, "We found Him! We found Him!" He was there all the time, but he needs to be in his rightful place; back in the manger. The Bible says, "You will seek me and find me when you seek me with all your heart." (Jeremiah 29:13 NIV).

The journey has begun, the seeking has started, and the finding is right under your nose so that all can see. Come on, we are just beginning, and we are on the right track. Grab your camels, take your sheep, and find a friend, for you too can exclaim, "I found Him!"

"This will be a sign to you: You will find a baby wrapped in cloths and lying in a manger." (Luke 2:12 NIV).

(And this taxing was first made when Cyrenius was governor of Syria.)

And all went out to be taxed, everyone to his own city.

Luke 2:2-3 (KJV)

Day Three
"Details of the Dubious Kind"

Now, before we continue our Christmas journey, I must give you some words of caution. Many of you know a lot about Christmas and its festivities, and you might find some of what I write as quite immature or trivial. You have taken the Christmas test at church and you know that there were not just three Wise Men, but we say there were three because they brought three kinds of gifts to the Christ-child: gold, frankincense, and myrrh. You also answered correctly when you said that the angels at Christmas did not sing, "Glory to God in the Highest…" for they only said it, and they did not sing it, and you were correct again. You know all the details of Christmas and the incidentals beside.

You know that Santa Claus originally came from Antalya, Turkey, and that there are two versions of "Away in the Manger."[2] You can tell with assurance that Emmanuel and Immanuel are just two spellings of the same name. You know all the details, both fact and fiction. In fact, you know that Caesar is like saying President and there were many kings or men called Caesar. No trivia, not a detail one, has passed your

---

[2] "Away in a Manger" is a Christmas song but whose source is unknown for stanzas 1,2, however John Thomas McFarland wrote stanza 3. But there are two musical versions of the song, one being called the "Cradle Song" and the other called, "Away in a Manger."

understanding. You are the Christmas King, the Official Christmas Tree Debutante, and Santa's Little Helper.

But there are few details you may have missed:

You know that Jesus was born in Bethlehem, but forgot why he was born.

You know that Jesus' mother was Mary, but forgot why she was chosen.

You know the shepherds came, but forgot the message that they spread upon their return.

It is like the first kiss you had as a youngster after practicing in the mirror and kissing the back of your hand. You had rehearsed it many times, but when it happened with sweaty palms and racing hearts, it was more than in the details. You had missed the point. It was not the scientific knowledge of puckered lips and the coordination of face muscles, but that first kiss was the essence of love and care that accompanied each desire.

That too is Christmas, with its many stories, songs, and trivia but it is understandably more than that, for we know that God coming to man is not a detail to be analyzed, but it is love to be accepted and a desire to be fulfilled.

Details? Yes, you may know them all, but have you experienced the essence of God's love and Christ's birth? It is not trivia, trivial, or the summation of all the facts. It is God! He has come, and He came to us. Creator to creation. God to man, and it happened on Christmas, and that detail we may never understand.

So, take his name, Emmanuel or Immanuel, and know that it means, "God with us." Us? Me? You? Yes, all of us, and He is still here living in us by his Holy Spirit. He is still with us.

"All of this took place to fulfill what the Lord had said through the prophets: "The virgin will be with child and will give birth to a son, and they will call him Immanuel" – which means, "God with us." (Matthew 1:23 NIV).

And Joseph also went up from Galilee, out of the city of Nazareth, into Judea, unto the city of David, which is called Bethlehem; (because he was of the house and lineage of David:)

To be taxed with Mary his espoused wife, being great with child.

Luke 2:4-5 (KJV)

Day Four
"Us with God"

Yesterday we left off with God being with us, coming to us, and residing with us for now and eternity. We are now in the Advent season, which will lead us into the Christmas festivities over the next four weeks and bring us to the full realization of what Emmanuel really means.

Everyone is beginning to get excited about God being here, the arrival of the Christ-child; here, right now, here in this world, but wait just a minute. Here today? Right now? It may not be as exciting as you think.

Let me tell you a quick story to emphasize the point. When I was a kid, my brother was asked many times by my parents to look out for me, babysit as they called it, and on this day it was no exception. Wherever he went, I went, I had to go. Whoever he saw, I saw, because I had to tag along. However, on this particular day, my brother's best friend, Vernon, had just bought a new Rambler convertible, and the car was, as some would say now a real, "chick magnet." But I was there, this "Leave It To Beaver"[3] brother, tagging along and saying stupid things, and looking the same way. They would say, "Let's go check out the girls," but then in the next breath, "But we have Rodney with us." I was in the way. They could

---

[3] Connelly, J., Mosher, B., Conway, D. (Producers). (1957-1963). *Leave it to Beaver* (Television Series). CBS/ABC, Los Angeles, California.

have changed their ways, but instead they changed their passenger and the next thing I knew, they had left me at Edward's house, and told me to stay put. They would be back later, much later.

In fact, most of the time, they did not want me around at all, or at least on those days of wanton lust. They would drop me off and pick me back up at their convenience. I was like a bad cold that never goes away.

Which brings us back to "Emmanuel." God is here and here all the time. It appears at times that we wish that we too could just drop off God for a while, especially when he is getting in the way, and then pick him up later when we needed him. "God with us," today? Now? Can't you come back tomorrow?

But the reality is, Jesus has already come over 2000 years ago, and he is here, and his Holy Spirit is directing us. He wants to be with you, so don't drop him off at your friend's house, don't kick him out of the car, or out of the bedroom, or leave him in another town, take him with you.

Today is only the start of the Christmas season, so over the next month and more, sing the hymn along with the angels…. ooh, we almost forgot that they did not sing, they only said the words, well, let us sing anyway, "O Come O Come, Emmanuel, and ransom captive Israel…." And mean it. "God with us" and "Us with God!" Then Christ will come and abide with us forever.

…and they shall call his name Emmanuel, which being interpreted is, God with us.

Matt. 1:23b (KJV)

Day Five
"Incarnation"

For the last two days we have examined the word, "Emmanuel" with some its ramifications. However, there are other Christmas words of theological implications that come up as well during the Christmas season that we must also examine. For example, take the word, "Incarnation," which is a lofty word heard in many Sunday sermons, a word heard, but not really understood. In theology, it means that Christ as God was incarnated, that is, God was made flesh and came into the world as man. It was an idea, a plan of such magnitude that it could only be conceived in the heart of God. It went from being a thought to being something concrete, something real during the Christmas season that can be seen and heard; a baby who can be touched and held, coddled and fed.

But incarnation also means, "That which personifies a quality or trait."[4] For example, "Bats are the incarnation of all that is evil and unclean," and if you have ever looked into the face of a bat, you will immediately understand that concept.

As I paused to think of this word, Incarnation, which is so often used in connection with Christmas, I began to wonder that if concepts, thoughts, and traits can

---

[4] Morris, W. (1976). *The American Heritage Dictionary of the English Language*. Boston: Houghton Mifflin Co,

be incarnated; made into bodily form, then why not emotions as well. What would emotions look like if they too were incarnated into something concrete, something tangible, real, not just felt? We express that at times, for we use phrases such as the "dove of peace,"," or "happy as a lark," or better yet, that "dumb dog of ours." Personality and emotion have become so interlinked with one thing or object that it comes to incarnate that one manifestation.

In fact, the Bible tells us that, "The Word became flesh and made his dwelling among us. We have seen his glory, the glory of the One and Only, who came from the Father, full of grace and truth." (John 1:14 NIV). What was that one Word, that essence of emotion seen and heard, that one personality trait that was born on Christmas Day? You see, emotions, have been incarnated, that is changed from a thought or feeling into a viable living organism, and if I asked you right now to answer the question, the question on my lips for all you readers to answer, you would know instantly, and you would all lift your hands and yell, "I know, I know. I know the emotion, the Word, that was born on Christmas Day. I know that LOVE was incarnated into Jesus for it says in the Bible that "God is love." (I John 4:16a NIV). "This is love: not that we love God, but, that he loved us and sent his Son...." (I John 4:10a NIV). It would be another A on your Christmas report card.

Love was sent to earth in a form, a body, a personification of all that we can know about love and it was found and was incarnated in the Christ-child. Is it no wonder that the Bible tells us, "When they had seen him, they spread the word concerning what had been told them about this child, and all who heard it were amazed

They had seen an emotion, an incarnation of love, living in front of their very eyes and it was amazing and still is. Jesus, the incarnate Word.

And so it was, that, while they were there, the days were accomplished that she should be delivered.

And she brought forth her firstborn son, and wrapped him in swaddling clothes, and laid him in a manger; because there was no room in the inn.

Luke 2:6-7 (KJV)

Day Six

"Supercalifragilisticexpialidocious"

By now, we are almost at the end of our first week of our "38" days of Christmas. You should have already begun to feel the expectation, the excitement building for the coming of Christmas and the birth of the Christ-child. We have learned already that emotions can be summed up in one word, a word that Jesus personifies: love. But there are still many other words used to describe the season we are in and you know where I am going with this one from the chapter title already given.

Our family has watched Julie Andrews in "Sound of Music"[5] and "Mary Poppins"[6] just one too many times, for we know and can sing, not dance, (not coordinated enough for that), to most of the songs. Once our family even took the "Sound of Music" tour while traveling through Salzburg, Austria. These movies have feel good music, energetic lyrics, and fun words, catchy words such as, "supercalifragilisticexpialidocious," (and my spell checker just went wild). They are words that youngsters love to say, such as the ole, "Peter Piper picked…." You get the picture.

---

[5] Wise, R. (Director). (1965). *Sound of Music* (Motion Picture). United States: 20th Century Fox

[6] Stevenson, R. (Director). (1964). *Mary Poppins* (Motion Picture). United States: Walt Disney Productions

And of course, there are other fun words that you hear, not only at this season, but also around various localities, whether it is southern slang or intercity jargon. Even when you are trying to learn a new language you learn to laugh at yourself as you answer the phone in Japanese with a "mooshe, mooshe," or how about the Turkish words, "soyle, boyle," the equivalent of the English, "okey, dokey." Again, there are the additional foreign words that your children learn and love to say just because they sound like something "nasty" in English. Your kids say them and then they hope to get out of trouble by saying it was an "Albanian" phrase. These are words you use, because they fit, they feel good, they make you laugh. Fun words, words you use over and over. Why? Just because you like the way it sounds and the flavor it adds to the conversation. They sound good to your ear.

Now you bet that I am going to tell you that the Bible has fun words too. It must, for God loves saying them and especially at Christmas. He loves to use the word, "glory" and "joy" along with "praise" and "good news." Christmas is a fun time and just yesterday, we learned that God's favorite word was love for that is who he is. He uses the word hundreds of times in the Bible. It just rolls off his tongue. It makes God feel so good and it is one of those words that makes you feel warm all over, so much so that I made up a new fun word that I am adding to the Christmas season:

"Superlovealotyouexpectitasyouhearit." Now if only I could find a good rooftop in London, a few chimney sweeps, and a good dance number to go along with it.

You see, Christmas is such a fun word and it brings so much to the dreary winter season, for as the angels proclaimed, "Do not be afraid. I bring you good news of great joy that will be for all people. Today in the town of David a Savior has been born to you; he is Christ the Lord." (Luke 2:10-11 NIV). Don't these words calm and soothe you, like sitting in your rocking chair around an open hearth with your lap blanket at your side, watching the lights twinkle on your Christmas tree with a fresh cup of tea in your hand…. Now that is soothing!

So, join with me and sing…. Let us sing another fun word. I have just made it up. I am really getting good at this.

"SuperChristmasdayishereandwereallydoenjoyit." Doesn't that feel good? You know it does, you have to admit it, you must, it's Christmas.

And there were in the same country shepherds abiding in the field, keeping watch over their flock by night.
And lo, the angel of the Lord came upon them, and the glory of the Lord shone round about them: and they were sore afraid.
Luke 2:8-9 (KJV)

Day Seven
"Psychobabble"

As we finish our first week of our journey on the "38" days of Christmas, I have begun to sense there will be more, much more to see and learn than I now know. I am beginning to see that the center of all things will be Christ. I see that I am trying to act different now, think different now, and behave differently.

A few weeks back I attended a workshop in behavioral transformation, a term that I really do not understand. Usually I go to these meetings knowing that I will pick up a few credits to maintain my counseling credentials, but not really giving the material a second thought. However, on this lesson, I really did learn something. The teacher informed us in her own words that, "Cognitive distortions occur when your mental filter, in awfulizing the occurring polarized ideation of deprivation in parental capacities causes a change in the Prochaska-DiClemente's[7] wheel of change and your ambivalence passively disengages your ability to actively listen." To which I say, "amen."

And then she added, just so that we could get in touch with our emotions, our inner self, "How does that

---

[7] Prochaska, J. & DiClemente, C. (1984) *The transtheoretical approach: crossing traditional boundaries of therapy*, Homewood, IL: Dow Jones-Irwin.

make you feel?" To which I replied in my mind, "Can I be excused to go to the bathroom?"

Although, I did learn some additional paradigms, so let me explain. I learned in the "Culture of Therapy," that you need:

1. Someone outside of yourself to help you solve problems.
2. Someone outside of yourself to provide you with answers.
3. Someone outside of yourself to help you get your goals in life.
4. Someone outside of yourself to educate your children properly.
5. Someone outside of yourself to know what you need.

Again, I say a resounding cry, "Yes." "Yes," to all those paradigms. I do need someone smarter than myself, better than I, and with way more wisdom.

But then the "other shoe fell" and the teacher informed us that she was talking about the government, social systems, and cultural norms. And on this point, I could not resist to say, "Culture does not define who I am, and I am not just a composite of statistics and charts.

Yes, we do need someone's help and we know that someone, we really do. The Bible states again that, "Today in the town of David a Savior has been born to you; he is Christ the Lord." (Luke 2:11NIV).

Christ, the Messiah, meaning the Anointed One, is the one who arrived on Christmas Day having known us from our mother's womb, and who calls us by name.

(John 10:3 KJV). He came to earth bearing good news to all of us and he has told all of creation that he loves me, he loves you, and is totally outside of ourselves. Why? Because he fits the paradigm of all that the world needs.

So, let me cognitively express my intervention strategy without consultation or critical thinking, in imagery that all can understand just as the angels did: Our Savior, our Messiah, our helper, our friend, and our teacher has filled in all the blanks in this culture of therapy. The Bible tells us that, "I bring you good news of great joy that will be for all the people… a **Savior**."

behavioral transformation, "Doesn't that make you really feel good?

And the angel said unto them, Fear not: for, behold, I bring you good tidings of great joy, which shall be to all people.

For unto you is born this day in the city of David a Saviour, which is Christ the Lord.

And this shall be a sign unto you; Ye shall find the babe wrapped in swaddling clothes, lying in a manger.

And suddenly there was with the angel a multitude of the heavenly host praising God, and saying,

Glory to God in the highest, and on earth peace, good will toward men.

Luke 2:10-14 (KJV)

Day Eight
"SAD"

We are now into our second week on our "38" day journey to Christmas. It is not winter yet, for it does not come until a couple of more weeks, but we are definitely experiencing the autumn breezes and the cooler temperatures. It is a favorite time for many for summer has passed, the trees are changing colors, and the mosquitoes are taking a vacation south.

However, seasonal change can cause a variety of other issues as we race towards winter, and some are good and some not so good. We experienced this at the mental health clinic that I used to work at. We made all the various diagnoses and applied the related acronyms: ADD, ADHD, ODD, PAD, and for sure the most widely used: ABCDEFGHIJKLMNOP. We saved the rest of the alphabet for those with more severe conditions. But there was one disorder that goes along with the change of seasons and the DSM[8] manual has labeled it appropriately; SAD. It stands for "Seasonal Affective Disorder" and of course it makes you just that-sad. It is just another name I think for the old "winter blues." It is mostly seen in areas where long winters and extended stays inside your home leads one to feelings of

---

[8] American Psychiatric Association. (2013). *Diagnostic and Statistical Manual of Mental Disorders,* (5th ed.). Washington D.C, USA: Author

depression and despair, with the only sure cure being the return of summer, or a quick move to South Florida.

Nevertheless, researchers have found that sitting in bright ultraviolet light can ease the depression and the symptoms of SAD and rightly so.

We have known for years that if you sit in light as opposed to staying in darkness, good things begin to happen. The light relieves some of the depression and concern and moves you into feelings of peace and harmony. Light even provides you with vitamin D and other essential nutriments that your body needs for growth and healing. Light, some would say, is another food group added to your fruits and vegetables.

So, isn't it remarkable that in the prophecies of Jesus' birth in the Old Testament, Isaiah tells us, "The people walking in darkness have seen a great light; on those living in the land of the shadow of death a light has dawned." (Isaiah 9:2 NIV). And in Luke it is recorded, "And there were shepherds living out in the fields nearby, keeping watch over their flocks at night. An angel of the Lord appeared to them, and the glory of the Lord shone around them…. (Luke 2:8-9a NIV) Light was the factor that heralded Jesus' birth. In fact, Jesus is called the "Light of the World," and in I Peter 2:9 (NIV) it goes on to say that Jesus has "…. called us out of darkness into his wonderful light." We now know that there is healing and health in sitting in the light of God's presence. Sitting in long periods of darkness leads us to disorientation and a lack of vision and direction, while sitting in the glory, in the light of Jesus' birth, takes you to the place of assurance and peace. He is our peace.

So today let us rejoice and celebrate God's goodness as the shepherds did, "The shepherds returned, glorifying God for all the things that they had heard and seen, which were just as had been told." (Luke 2:20 NIV). They had seen the light and the glory, and you too can bask in his light and move out of your darkness. You can chase the blues away and laugh at your friend's tired Christmas jokes. You can be cured, released, and renewed, and you can stop being SAD, Christmas is here.

And it came to pass to pass, as the angels were gone into heaven, the shepherds said to one another, Let us now go even unto Bethlehem, and see this thing which is to come to pass, which the Lord hath made known unto us.

And they came with haste, and found Mary, and Joseph, and the babe lying in a manger.

And when they had seen it, they made known abroad the saying which was told them concerning the child.

And all they that heard it wondered at those things which were told them by the shepherds.

Luke 2:15-18 (KJV)

Day Nine
"Manatees and Platypuses"

I know it is only the second week of our "38" day journey to Christmas and already I am confused, however, not sad, as I wrote about yesterday. My mind is going non-stop, and I am trying to concentrate on the Christ-child. I am looking for this "Peace on Earth," but it is sure hard to find, and by Christmas I will be a basket case of random thoughts if I don't get a grip on this holiday season. So, I have got to concentrate, and that is just what I will do. Concentrate. Concentrate. I know what I can do. I can practice one of my counseling, "tricks of the trade" techniques that I learned in Psychology 101. They tell you that it is psychologically impossible to think of two things at the same time. You just cannot do it. If you are describing in your mind an elephant with its big ears and long trunk and you visualize the elephant standing in the jungle with her young one at her side, you cannot at the same time think of a camel with its wooly hair and one hump, or two, if you are wearing bifocals, standing in the Sahara Desert.

You must do this: Your mind must stop thinking about the elephant and then refocus your mind on your knowledge of camels and their physical characteristics, or otherwise you will throw yourself into a schizophrenic breakdown. It will cause you confusion and then your mind will cause you to think about the duck-billed platypus, an animal of epic confusion.

And that my friend is where I have already gone in my thinking about Christmas. It is no wonder that I and others like me are thrown into a state of bi-polar irregularity. I hear music telling me that, "Santa Claus is coming to town," while at the same time voices are calling out to me to sing, "Away in a manger no crib for his bed." My mind is trying to get Santa Claus on Joseph's knee with Mary hanging up her stocking. The chipmunks are singing to the sheep and one of the cows called Alvin,[9] is catching the Christmas train. Charlie Brown[10] in decorating the manger with this stressed tree and the Hallmark Channel is running non-stop reruns of "The Christmas Carol."[11] My mind cannot take it and I feel I must concentrate on just one thing.

I know what I can do, I am just going to sit and relax with the paper and a hot cup of tea, but what? Here in the middle of the page, aaaaah!!! There in the paper is an ad that reads, "Peace on Earth, Good Will Toward Manatees," an ad which was placed irreverently by some club in Florida. What am I going to do?

I know I am going to concentrate on just one thing if I can, so I put the paper down and picked up my Bible again, and read once more, "a Savior has been born to you." (Luke 2:11NIV). A Savior, yes, for the Bible says

[9] Bagdasarian, R. (Executive Producer). (1958) *David Seville and the Chipmunks* (Song), Los Angeles, Ca., USA: Jet Records

[10] Melendez, B. (Executive Producer). (1965). *A Charlie Brown Christmas* (Television Broadcast), Los Angeles, Ca.: CBS/Lee Mendelson Films

[11] Donner, C. (1984*). The Christmas Carol* (Television Movie). New York, New York: CBS

that Christ came into the world to save sinners. (I Timothy 1:15 NIV). I got it, I got it. I guess I just need to continue to concentrate on Jesus, my Savior, for to be honest, I have never saw a manatee that sinned, but then again, I have not met many manatees personally. But I am not from Florida but maybe Christmas should Manateemas, but I don't really think so…. concentrate, concentrate. You can do it.

So, I have decided to take my own advice and think only about one thing: the Christ-child. My thoughts are going to center on the baby, Jesus. I will regain my sanity and dwell on just one thing at a time and let the other thoughts go. The Bible tells me a "double minded man, unstable in all his ways," (James 1:8 KJV), and that is not what I want to be.

Manatees, platypuses, elephants, or camels? No, I think I will stick with the babe wrapped in swaddling clothes and lying in a manger. It works, it really works, doesn't it? I am cured, thank God.

But Mary kept all these things, and pondered them in her heart.

And the shepherds returned, glorifying and praising God for all the things that they had heard and seen, as it was told unto them.

Luke 2:19-20 (KJV)

Day Ten
"God of the Unexpected"

I would love to say I know how the ending of this book will turn out, but I really do not know. I expect one thing, but my expectations seemingly fall short. It's like the first Christmas and things were happening that no one could explain. They came out of nowhere, not seen before or since, not by Mary, nor by Joseph, and certainly not by the shepherds. But God is that way. He is a very creative God, and the Christ-child and the circumstances concerning his birth was a well laid plan. In fact, it is kind of comical; a king in a manger, a shepherd as a prophet, and a pregnant girl of 16, the bearer of the Messiah. Who would have expected?

It reminded me of another time when God unexpectedly showed up, and it too came in a comical way. It was back in my home state in Louisiana. We had traveled together as a youth group to Fisher, Louisiana, to a small church called Moss Bluff. It was the Friday night youth rally when all the small churches in the neighborhood got together so that the youth could meet, socialize, find a friend, and in my case, possibly find a girlfriend.

We had settled into the pews and were singing that old country favorite, "I'll Fly Away,"[12] when right past the second verse of the song, a tiny mouse got caught in

---

[12] Brumley, A. (1932). *I'll Fly Away* (Song). Hartford Music Co.

the floor fan and like a trapeze artist, he came flying through the air. In slow motion the whole church watched, as the mouse in fear came to a resting place right in the middle of the church, and with precision, next to the precocious teenage girls. That was all that was needed to turn the church service from a funeral dirge to singing the "Hallelujah" chorus. It was totally unexpected and totally unforgettable. However, it was a real God thing for no one could have coordinated the song, the mouse, the group of teenage girls, and the fan to be totally in sic. The timing was perfect, but unexpected.

Unexpected, not exactly like when your wife first whispered, "I'm pregnant," or when the boss called you in and all you hear is, "You're fired." At these unexpected times, you gasp and blink your eyes, and hope it was just a blip in time, but God is the God of the unexpected.

In Luke it says that Mary was expecting a child, and "While they were there, the time came for the baby to be born, and she gave birth to her firstborn, a son. She wrapped him in cloths and placed him in a manger, because there was no room for them in the inn." (Luke 2:6-7 NIV).

Yes, she was expecting, but she did not know what her expectations would bring. She was expecting a baby and she got the Messiah. She was expecting her firstborn but got a new king for a whole new kingdom. It was all in God's timing and it was perfect. Christmas is always like that, for you endeavor to plan and arrange, but when God takes over, the Christmas Day takes on a whole new perspective.

You know, I am an avid church attendee, but I do wish God would do something at church this Christmas totally unexpected. Church becomes predictable and stale. You know that Bro. Williams is going to get a coughing spell, and Jimmy, the 10-year-old, is going to make a scene running to the bathroom for the 6th time. But wait, wait until God tries to get our attention and out of the mundane, he unexpectedly interrupts the service and the wonder of awe sets in.

I am not praying this Christmas for a mouse to come unexpectedly, or a snake for that matter, but I am praying for God to bring the power of singing angels, and new births, and even a healing of Bro. Williams' coughing and a cure for Jimmy's incontinence. I am praying, from the pastor to the song leader, and to the child asleep in the pew, that we would all experience the unexpected presence of God, his glory and be amazed. Expect it.

And when the days of her purification according to the law of Moses were accomplished, they brought him to Jerusalem, to present him to the Lord;

(As it is written in the law of the Lord, Every male that openeth the womb shall be called holy to the Lord;)

And to offer a sacrifice according to that which is said in the law of the Lord, A pair of turtledoves, or two young pigeons.

Luke 2:22-24 (KJV)

Day Eleven
"Can I Get a Witness"

By now, the women have bought all their Christmas gifts and the men are still waiting for Christmas Eve to buy theirs. Men love shopping as much as a migraine on a hot summer day. It is just something we hate to do. I do not know if we don't like spending money or we just don't like spending money on anyone except ourselves. I will poll the women and let you know.

Which brings me to a story my wife loves to tell, but I deny it every time. One of her favorite tales, like an old wives' tale, is the story of the time we went Christmas shopping just after we were newly married. I hate shopping, but I had reluctantly agreed to go with my wife and my Mom over to the Mall in Alexandria. After about five minutes of, "Do you like this?" and "What do you think?" as she went through dresses one by one, I knew that I had to find a place to hide and kill time.

Just a few feet away was the perfect place. It was quiet, no one could see me, and as they turned their backs, I crawled up underneath one of those circular garment racks and proceeded to fall asleep. Thirty minutes later my Mom and my wife noticed that there was a man whose feet were sticking out from under the rack, in fact, he was also asleep and snoring and to their demise, he had on my shoes. "Wait a minute," he has on Rodney's pants as well, and then they understood, "It's Rodney!"

It was somewhat embarrassing to my wife and to this day, I deny it. I deny that it was as bad as she says, but she always has a comeback, "I have a witness, your Mom." "She saw you too." And then if my Mom is around, she begins to tell her story and finish off with her version for she was a witness to the entire event.

My wife then quotes the Bible, (just to make it spiritual and to rub it in) and she reads where the Bible talks of confirming an accusation in the presence of two or three witnesses, and I guess my wife and my Mom, "fit the bill." I am guilty, and I know it.

I guess there are a few others who are also guilty this Christmas. There were witnesses on that first Christmas Day. There were the shepherds, the angels, Mary and Joseph, the animals, the innkeeper, and the list goes on.

Historians such as Josephus, tell us about Christ, and the early church fathers gave their testimonies as well, along with the disciples and Jesus' followers, and about two billion Christians around the world. They all give their witness that something happened on that day and it's undeniable.

Archaeology and real science also are witnesses to the events of that day and if that is not enough, even the Holy Spirit of God gives a witness to our hearts.

So, I beg of you all, even the women who are reading this, to stop "shopping" around for another answer to Christmas and all its significance. Millions know Christ is real, and they know Christmas is coming, and you know it too.

"When they had seen him, they spread the word concerning what had been told them about this child," (Luke 2:18 NIV). They were witnesses and couldn't wait to tell. They saw the Christ-child, and so can you. You can be a witness to the entire Christmas story.

And, behold, there was a man in Jerusalem, whose name was Simeon; and the same man was just and devout, waiting for the consolation of Israel: and the Holy Ghost was upon him.

And it was revealed unto him by the Holy Ghost, that he should not see death, before he had seen the Lord's Christ.

And he came by the Spirit into the temple: and when the parents brought in the child Jesus, to do for him after the custom of the law,

The took he him up in his arms, and blessed him God, and said,

Lord, now lettest thou thy servant depart in peace, according to thy word:

For mine eyes have seen they salvation,

Which thou hast prepared before the face of all people;

A light to lighten the Gentiles, and the glory of thy people Israel.

Luke 2:25-32 (KJV)

Day Twelve
"What Would You do Without Xmas?"

I do not know, but I hope by now you are thinking about the coming of Christmas. But the question I want us to look at today is, "What would do without Christmas, and what would do if they left Christ out and all you had was the X?" There have been movies and plays that have explored that option, but none brought it home to me more than a funeral that I attended in Philadelphia.

A good pastor friend of mine, Pastor H., paid the ultimate price that day in ministry to the inner city, for his beautiful daughter had been tragically killed on the streets of Philly. It was a sad day for the entire community. It was eerie. I did not understand the how, much less the why. Later after the funeral, he quietly made the statement to me, "I do not know what I would do without Jesus." He was talking about the comfort and peace he felt, while I was still struggling with my own doubts as I tried to figure it all out.

However, it started me thinking. What would I do without Jesus? What would the world look like if Christ had not come? What would people feel if Christmas was just a fantasy of historical novels? What would I do if I did not have Jesus in my life?

"What would you do?"

So, I began to make a list of things in my head on what I would do if I did not have Jesus as my Lord and Savior. I made a list of things that would be different if there was no Christmas Day.

1. I would worry a lot and spend sleepless nights trying to understand the world.
2. I would fear death and never attend funerals again, for they would remind me of my frailty.
3. I would trust no one and would be constantly looking over my shoulder for some hint of danger.
4. I would suspect all my friends of sinister motives, for they had disappointed me too many times in the past. I know their hearts.
5. I would be angry at life for its ups and downs.
6. I would be depressed from that anger.
7. I would seek to be entertained to be happy for I would possess no happiness from within.
8. I would be addicted, for I would seek lasting pleasures in all the wrong places.
9. I would try to believe only in me, and I would disappoint myself.

I am sure you too would have a list as long as mine, filled with fear and regret.

In fact, if we really did not have Jesus, we would be miserable, and we would hate ourselves for having ever been born. But today, we can stand with my pastor friend and even in times of bitterness and loss know the joy of Christ's presence. So, "Do not be afraid. I bring you good news of great joy...." (Luke 2:10a NIV), and as the King James version of the Bible says, "Glory to God in the

highest, and on earth, peace goodwill toward men."
(Luke 2:14KJV).

Yes, Pastor H., "What would we do without Jesus, without Christmas?" I guess not much of anything, and thanks for reminding us all again to never be without the peace of our Lord in our lives. May God bless you.

And Joseph and his mother marveled at those things which were spoken of him.

And Simeon blessed them, and said unto Mary his mother, Behold, this child is set for the fall and rising again of many in Israel; and for a sign which shall be spoken against;

(Yea, a sword shall pierce through thy own soul also,) that the thoughts of many hearts may be revealed.

Luke 2:33-35 (KJV)

Day Thirteen
"Spitting into the Wind"

Yesterday, the thought for the day got a little depressing, but I am sorry, but this Christmas journey does have its ups and downs. I know it is Merry Christmas, but today my mind is still thinking about yesterday's thought and the futility of it all. If all there is, is what we see at Christmas; the tree, the shopping, and a few songs around an open fire, then it is a Dreary Christmas not a Merry Christmas and as the expression goes, "It is just spitting into the wind." Not my thought or expression, nor is it the best Christmas slogan, but it is one that I was awakened to by a visit to the dentist, and it is biblical, trust me.

I was sitting at the dentist's office waiting for my yearly check-up and reading those magazines that really thrill you, "USDA Food Facts" and "Oral Hygiene and You." There were a few others as well, but one caught my eye and it is bestseller I am sure, "Spitting into the Wind, The Facts about Dip and Chew."[13] And you think I am not an avid reader?

I missed this read last Christmas, but upon catching up on all the facts of "spitless tobacco" or "smokeless tobacco," I learned that that not only was it addictive, but

---

[13] U.S. Department of Health and Human Service, Public Health Service, National Institutes of Health. (2000). *Spitting into the Wind.* USA.

it also wears out the back pocket of your blue jeans, and if you dip, you will have to buy your yearly pair of Levi's again this Christmas.

I even brought the booklet home for my wife to read just in case she was thinking of trying a, "chaw."

But you know the Bible does say something about all of this…. really. In the latest contemporary translation of the book of Ecclesiastes, Solomon, the author of the book wrote, "Then I took a good look at everything I'd done, looked at all the sweat and hard work. But when I looked, I saw nothing but smoke. Smoke and 'spitting into the wind.' There was nothing to any of it. Nothing." (Ecclesiastes 2:11 The Message).

Solomon, the richest man to have ever lived and the wisest as well came to the point where he said, "I hate life." (Ecclesiastes 2:17 The Message). He had palaces and gold, women and wine, but he ended up in despair and in depression. He saw everything as just 'spitting into the wind,' and he was not talking of "spitless tobacco" either.

At the end, the author out of skepticism, comes to a wise conclusion, and that is, there is nothing that really matters in life except to, "Fear God. Do what he tells you." (Ecclesiastes 12:13 The Message).

You see without God coming to us this Christmas season, there is only mindless consumerism, greed, money, and festive parties. Then after that, nothing is left at all. Nothing has any meaning.

I am sure you will want more than just smoke, and 'spitting into the wind,' you will want to see Christmas in all its glory. You will want to know your King and Savior, your brother, and your friend. You will want to sit down and read your children the Christmas story. You will watch the "Jesus" movie and turn your hearts and minds to something more meaningful. You will take a fruitcake to your obnoxious neighbor and invite your mother-in-law to the Christmas table and even give her a chair to sit on. She got a little upset last year when she had to sit on the floor with the kids.

No, this year it is going to be different. This is going to be a "Merry Christmas" and a "Happy New Year." No ifs, ands, or buts, and no 'spitting into the wind.'

Isaiah wrote that this Christ, this Messiah, will be called, …. Wonderful, Counselor, Mighty God, Everlasting Father, Prince of Peace. (Isaiah 9:6 KJV). We can experience something that is more than nothing; something mighty, something wonderful, something everlasting, and something peaceful, and that something is our God, and that is nothing to "sneeze about" (now I wonder if that phrase is in the Bible too.)

And there was one Anna, a prophetess, the daughter of Phanuel, of the tribe of Aser: she was of great age, and had lived with an husband seven years from her virginity;

And she was a widow of about fourscore and four years, which departed not from the temple, but served God with fastings and prayers night and day.

Luke 2:36-37 (KJV)

Day Fourteen
"We're Not Dead Yet"

After a couple of days of feeling the loss of Christmas, I think we should go back and explore again the "joys" of Christmas. Awhile back, we had family night at church and we watched the movie, "Mom's Night Out," which I highly recommend. It is a movie about four women on a quest to take the night off from the children and just enjoy themselves, but since the movie is a comedy, the evening turns into a night filled with catastrophe and mayhem as the four women go from misstep to another. It is a "chick-flick," but one that the whole family can enjoy.

However, what I really enjoyed was sitting in the back of the church and watching the congregation laugh together, eat hot dogs together, and be happy in the Lord. We are always praying together and working together, but that night they were laughing together and just enjoying the movie and each other's company, and that was priceless.

We forget at the beginning of Christ's life, the angels said that Jesus' birth itself would bring good news and joy that will be to all people. (Luke 2:10). There is joy in knowing Jesus. I am not talking about silly laughter, the kind that comes from racial slurs and course jesting, but I am talking about joy that causes one to smile and laugh, step higher, and be glad in heart.

We forget that Jesus later in his life preached on joy and happiness as he taught us the Beatitudes to be happy or blessed. He taught us:

"Blessed (Happy) are the poor in spirit…."

"Blessed (Happy) are the pure in heart…"

"Blessed (Happy) are the merciful…"

"Blessed (Happy) are the peacemakers" … the mournful, and even the persecuted…. (Matthew 5:3-10 NIV)

Jesus reminds us that there are so many things to be happy for. In fact, that joy can be expressed at home, at work, and even at church while watching an entertaining movie.

I thought it quite funny the other day when a famous secular singing group came through town, and I saw some of our church members there clapping their hands and tapping their toes, and they are the same ones that always complain on Sunday morning and refuse to enter into a song of lively music. Clap? In church? No way. It would be sacrilegious.

But you do not have to be that way. We can sing about Christmas joy and clap our hands as well, and even lift our hands in church to express it. As the singer, Larry Norman,[14] said in one of his songs, "I don't like any of those funeral marches, I ain't dead yet."

---

[14] Larry Norman (4.8.1947 – 2.24.2008) was a musician, singer, songwriter, and record producer. Considered to be the "Father" of Christian Rock Music.

So, this Christmas, laugh, smile, and love. You may be old, sick, but you are not dead, so express your happiness to our God. Why should satan have all the funny lines at Christmas and all the good jokes, and again as Larry Norman entitled one of his songs, "Why Should the Devil have all the Good Music?"[15] for he doesn't.

Therefore, this Christmas, grab a tall glass of iced tea, a hotdog, and watch a clean funny Christmas movie with your friends and family and relax in the presence of your God and King. It is fun and a real joy, and remember, "You ain't dead yet."

And she coming in that instant gave thanks likewise unto the Lord, and spoke of him to all them that looked for redemption in Jerusalem.

And when they had performed all things according to the law of the Lord, they returned into Galilee, to their own city Nazareth.

And the child grew, and waxed strong in spirit, filled with wisdom: and the grace of God was upon him.

Luke 2:38-40 (KJV)

---

[15] Norman, L. (1969) *Why should the devil have all the good music?* (Song). Los Angeles, Ca. USA: Capital Records

Day Fifteen
"A Turtle, A Frog, and a Lizard"

It is interesting as we study and delve into all the nuances of the Christmas story that sometimes there is just a word or two that help us to see and understand the holiday season in another way. In Luke 2:15, it reads, "When the angels left them and gone into heaven, the shepherds said to one another, "Let's go to Bethlehem and see this thing that has happened, which the Lord told us about."

Do you see? Did you catch it? The shepherds in plural, said to one another, let **us,** and see what was told **us.** They saw in the plural, not the singular. No one was left out. As we come to Christmas, we too must understand that the Bible is an "Us" book, not a "Me" book. Remember when the disciples asked Jesus to teach them to pray, the prayer begins with "Our" Father, and the prayer asks to lead us, deliver us, give us, and forgive us. The Bible is a collective book starting back at the creation beginning with Genesis as God expresses the act of creation with, "Then God said, Let us make man in our image.... (Genesis 1:26a KJV) It was act of the trinitarian God relating as "us."

But let me further illustrate this with a quirky story of sorts. If you had known my father, you would have known a rather eccentric man, the mad professor type. He loved biology and old cars and had fused these two joys together in his classic Plymouth Barracuda, for he had added a few biological extras, some accessories, just to make it his own. He had glued a dried-up frog, a dead turtle complete with shell, and an equally unresponsive lizard onto the dashboard of his car. They stayed there for years and when my father passed away, I removed them and have kept them in my desk up to this day.

I use them from time to time in sermon illustrations to try and make a point. These three were the best of buddies and I want to make sure they stay together as friends. You see, these reptiles have car pooled to work side by side for years. They have gone on vacation together and they even got a tan together lying under the hot sun in Louisiana. Similarly, they went to the same school, to the same church, week after week, day after day. They enjoyed the ride for they were comrades in arms, fellow students, alumni, but sad to say, they never became friends.

They had been so close, but they never spoke a word, never communicated a line, never even said hi. They never moved out of their comfort zone, they couldn't for they were glued to the dashboard, but don't get technical, I'm trying to make a point.

They had names like Hi and Hey, and You, but the relationship only went that far. If they were to ever be friends, communication had to go further than that. To be a true friend, one must express himself and share one's heart, and that never happened to them.

You see, Christmas is an "us" event that must be shared, talked about, and together in unity be celebrated. You cannot do church alone, you cannot do Christmas alone, and you cannot be friends alone without communication and fellowship taking place. So, quit being "say hi" friends and let **us** together sing, proclaim, and tell the Christmas story to all those around and call them friends. Come on friends, let's talk. It is more than you, more than me, but it is not more than us.

Now when Jesus was born in Bethlehem of Judea in the days of Herod the king, behold, there came wise men from the east of Jerusalem,

Saying, Where is he that is born King of the Jews? for we have seen his star in the east, and are come to worship him.

When Herod the king had heard these things, he was troubled, and all Jerusalem with him.

And when he had gathered all the chief priests and scribes of the people together, he demanded of them where the Christ should be born.

Matthew 2:1-4 (KJV)

Day Sixteen
"Giving in Waste"

We are past the second week and are now counting the days until the December 25th Christmas Day. Again, men, it is time to start thinking of a gift, for you only have until Christmas Eve, and women, you still have time to put something on lay-a-way. I know it is not the gift, but the spirit behind the giving, but you married men, you know by now, something needs to be under the tree soon.

Recently, some of my friends came over to visit and we were discussing our Christmas gifts and what we had and had not bought. My friend commented that he always buys his wife a jewelry item for every major holiday, a comment that my wife heard and insisted that I follow as well, as she gazed at the newly purchased vacuum cleaner with all its accessories. It is better than the dustpan and broom that I bought the year before.

At first, when my friend talked of his diamond purchases, I thought how frivolous and reckless that you would continue to buy gifts that have no practical value. A gift that not only reduces your wallet, but one that doesn't make coffee as well.

I found myself acting like Judas at the time when the woman, Mary, not the mother of Jesus, but, Mary the sister of Martha, anointed Jesus with expensive perfume to the point of waste. (John 12:1-7 NIV). Objecting to the fact that this pint of perfume could have been sold and used in a more rational way, Judas is rebuked by Jesus for not understanding the nature and spirit behind the giving of the perfume. She had given wastefully and without practicality.

As one writer says, "The highest form of giving is giving in waste." Giving that makes no sense except that love compels you to give and give again. Not out of need or want, nor out of duty or demand, but a gift given only to bring honor and love to the one who receives it and joy to the one who gives.

Mary in just a few fleeting minutes of sacrifice had given to Jesus an anointing of compassion that reached into the depths of time. An eternal gift, given to us as an example of care and concern for all to follow.

At Christmas, we talk of gifts and we all give, and so did everyone on that first Christmas day. The shepherds gave gifts of praise and glorified God, giving what they had at that very moment. Later the Wise Men gave gifts of great financial expense to the Christ-child who had no idea of their worth. I ask, "What two-year-old understands the nature of gold and precious spices?" But they were given in waste out of a heart filled with compassion.

We too can give gifts to God, not that he needs anything, but we need to know the secret of a giving heart. We can always give gifts of honor and love, gifts of praise and adoration, and gifts beyond the practical and useful. The shepherds understood, the Wise Men understood, and Mary, Martha's sister, understood as well.

This year, give God more than you are, more than you have, and more than you can. Give it all and then some, in fact, give God your whole heart. It's Christmas and a time for giving, a time to waste.

And they said unto him, In Bethlehem of Judea: for thus it is written by the prophet,

And thou Bethlehem, in the land of Juda, art not the least among the princes of Juda: for out of thee shall come a Governor, that shall rule my people Israel.

Then Herod, when he had privily called the wise men, inquired of them diligently what time the star appeared. And he sent them to Bethlehem, and said, Go and search diligently for the young child; and when ye have found him, bring me word again, that I may come and worship him also.

When they had heard the king, they departed; and, lo, the star, which they saw in the east, went before them, till it came and stood over there the young child was.

Matthew 2:5-9 (KJV)

Day Seventeen
"Feasting"

Yesterday we examined giving to others in waste and it seemed a little over the top. But I am here to remind you again that Christmas should be celebrated over the top, over the top of all holidays, marriages, and even birthdays. It is the holiday season and less than a month ago, we celebrated Thanksgiving and we feasted to excess, like the Duke and Duchess of Exeter, and the King of Siam.

But there are other feasts that are celebrated each autumn as well. There are the Fall Festivals, office parties, and of course festivals or feasts taken direct from the Old Testament. There were in September, the Feast of Tabernacles (Sukkot), the Feast of Trumpets (Rosh Hashanah), and Yom Kippur, and now in December there is the Festival of Lights (Chanukah). I am not Jewish, but I do appreciate much of the symbolism that goes into each feast and festival.

Later next year, there will be Spring feasts such as Passover and Pentecost, and many more that commemorate events both past and present, but one thing that strikes me most is that most are all called, "feasts." They are not some insignificant sandwich bought at the local deli, or a potato salad purchased at the supermarket, these are times over the top, days of excess, doing more than we normally do. They are not all feasts in the classic sense of eating to gluttonous misfortune, no, they are events that compel us to do more, to think more, to act more, and to give move of ourselves.

When I think of the celebrations in the Christian circles, it would be good if we reexamined our significant events and gave them greater value and a magnitude that reflects their importance. We take the Lord's Supper where we reflect on the magnitude of God and we do so with a thimbleful of juice and a minuscule wafer. What kind of celebration is that? Where is the feast?

We have just eaten our Thanksgiving meal last month and soon we will celebrate Christmas, but where are the feasts? Where is the greatness of God, the colossal God of the universe? We invite him for a day, and we pray over the meal and then we continue on. Just like at Communion, we quickly swallow the bread and wash it down with a sip of juice and go on our way.

No, I think we need to have a Thanksgiving Feast, a Christmas Feast, and even the Lord's Supper Feast, and while we are at it, let us invent a few more. We have made God too small.

Therefore, as the light of God's *greatness* shone on Christmas Day and the *great* company of the heavenly host were present for Jesus' birth, together with *amazing* things that were happening, why not feast this Christmas, not just for one day, but maybe for the entire "38" days of Christmas. What a time that would be! It is going way over the top and rightly so.

When they saw the star, they rejoiced with exceeding great joy.

Matthew 2:10 (KJV)

Day Eighteen
"Peace on Earth"

We are now beginning to feast on Christmas, carols are playing, Santa is ringing his bell in front of the Mall, and a spirit of Christmas is hanging in the air. It's Christmas, that day where the angels first proclaimed in earnest, "Peace on Earth." However, this evening when I turned on the nightly news, peace was nowhere to be found. I began to cry out, "Why doesn't God do something?" It is just not fair. All those starving children and God does nothing. Where is God when you need him? I pray and pray and pray, and still it seems nothing changes. It is downright awful. Crime is on the rise and sickness abounds, racism flourishes, and hate increases, and still God remains silent. It is like he does not care, for if God cared, he would do something about all this mess.

Well, He Has!

Don't you see, many times God does not need to answer a prayer because he has given you the ability to answer it. Out of most prayers we petition, we are the ones who can make the difference, and we can answer our own prayers. We pray for starving children, then feed them. We pray for the sick, then visit and care for them, and then anoint them for their healing. We pray for those who have never heard the good news of the gospel, then go and tell them. We pray for the uneducated and illiterate of the world, then help to build schools and universities. We pray for a green earth and a more advantageous society, then plant a tree and share a smile.

At this moment, this Christmas, we do pray, and we do pray for all those things mentioned above, but what about, "peace on earth?" How about peace in the Middle East? How about peace in our inner cities, and peace in rural America plagued by drugs? Ataturk,[16] the famous politician and father of the Turkish Republic, wisely stated, "Peace at home, Peace in the world." But of course, he forgot the most important aspect of peace that you must have before true peace can come, and that is, we must have "peace in our hearts." Ataturk should have said, "Peace in our heart, Peace at home, and Peace in the World."

However, this peace can never be found until you come to know this Christmas child, who came to be known as the, "Prince of Peace," for the scriptures say, "Peace I leave with you; my peace I give you. I do not give to you as the world gives. Do not let your hearts be troubled and do not be afraid." (John 14:27 NIV).

It is the same message given on Christmas day when the angels said to the shepherds, "Do not be afraid…" (Luke 2:10 NIV), for the angels were proclaiming that the peace of God was coming into this world through the birth of this tiny baby, Jesus.

So, let us look again. We can answer our own prayers for the starving, the poor, the sick, and even the planet, but you know we cannot answer the prayer asking for

---

[16] Kemal Ataturk is considered to be the "Father" of the present day, Republic of Turkey.

peace, only God can do that. God can begin by bringing peace in our hearts, our minds, our very being, and with that being stated, we can share that peace for all the world to hear. "Peace on earth, Good will toward man," and "May the Peace of the Lord be upon you all." And everyone said, "Amen."

And when they were come into the house, they saw the young child with Mary his mother, and fell down, and worshipped him: and when they had opened their treasures, they presented unto him gifts; gold, and frankincense, and myrrh.

And being warned of God in a dream that they should not return to Herod, they departed into their own country another way.

Matthew 2:11-12 (KJV)

Day Nineteen
"Let's Talk about Babes"

Now before you close the book and think I am going to talk about the "Babes" on the beach or the "Babes" at your work, I am here to inform you we are going to center on the "Babe, wrapped in swaddling clothes and lying in a manger." (Luke 2:12 KJV). It is a word used in the South frequently but usually taken out of context.

Just yesterday I was at a local grocery store and the lady began, "Thank you, Babe," as the woman took my dollar and gave me some change. "Babe," I thought, why I am not even your friend, especially not your babe; at least as far I know. But this sort of thing happens a lot in the South and it sometimes worries me.

Then again, just this afternoon, I was ordering a hamburger from the local hamburger "joint," when the cashier answered, "That will be $7.64, hon." "Hon?" Why I don't even know you, I mean, my wife is going to think we have something going on if you keep calling me honey.

Babe, Honey, and then there was the older sales lady at the shoe store who looked about my age, that when I asked her if she could help me find shoes in size 10, she simply said, "Well, I will check on that, Sweetie."

"Sweetie?" Just like the others, she did not even know my name either, and she kept calling me those terms of endearment. I was impressed, but really my name is Rodney, like Rodney Dangerfield, you get the picture, and I hope you know that I say that in jest. I was flattered, until I noticed she called everyone else, "Sweetie" as well.

I know we do this all the time, and we do it to God as well. We call him the "Man Upstairs" and "The big guy in the sky." We use terms that do not give him much honor and at times we even curse in his name. If you want to curse someone, curse the devil, for he deserves it for all the evil he has done.

All throughout the world, many who do not know God by name, make up names for God that sound flattering and impressive, when all we have to so is read the Christmas story and know that his real name is, "Jesus." I guess on Christmas day you could call him, "Babe" since he was a babe in the manger, but something is missing in that connotation, as well as in many other names people use to fill in the blanks.

But we know that God does have a name and he has revealed that name or names to us. As we learned earlier, he is called Immanuel, The Christ, The Messiah, but the name he really likes to be called by you is, "Lord." He wants to be the Lord of your life, the Lord of your family, and the Lord of the universe. He is really called, Jesus our Lord, and that name is above all names.

In the next couple of days, we will look at the name of our Lord, because we are getting closer and closer to Christmas and we do not want to call him; it, or "The God as you see Him", or anything less than He deserves.

So, this week remember when you meet the lady at the supermarket, tell her, "Sweetie, his name is Jesus, and Hon, I just wanted you to know that, and Babe…." You had better stop there or else your wife or husband will be calling you names that will not bear repeating. Just remember that the Christmas Babe is really Jesus your Lord.

And when they were departed, behold, the angel of the Lord appeareth to Joseph in a dream, saying, Arise, and take the young child and his mother, and flee into Egypt, and be thou there until I bring thee word: for Herod will seek the young child to destroy him.

When he arose, he took the young child and his mother by night, and departed into Egypt:

And was there until the death of Herod: that it might be spoken of the Lord by the prophet, saying, Out of Egypt have I called my son.

Matthew 13-15 (KJV)

Day Twenty
"Step-Father's Day"

Up to now, we have been learning about Mary, the Shepherds, the Wisemen, and of course, Jesus, but we have left Joseph to fend for himself on the sidelines. So today we are going to celebrate "Step-Father Day" or "Joseph's Day" for you all know that Joseph was not Jesus' real father in the biological sense, but only his step-father. Today, we are going down the path of masculinity and manhood and to a word you usually do not hear when talking about men: humility.

So, let me begin "Joseph's Day" with a delightful story. I lived in a town with a huge population of RVers, (people who live in recreational vehicles), and whether in Phoenix for the winter or in Maine for the summer, these group of the elderly and retired were some of the most interesting people that you will ever meet. Many live in their RVs all year and as you step inside you will see a reflection of all they hold dear to their hearts. They are a precious people.

In the town where I served, I would hold church services for members of the RV community and I fondly remember one residence in particular. He was an 87-year-old man who could not drive anymore, living by himself as a widower, but who walked up and down the lane each day greeting everyone and just being nice, and he went by the name of Mr. Hagan. He had no place to go, but he attended church faithfully each Sunday and he informed

56

me he had given his life to Jesus as age 12 and had continually lived for the Lord for all these years. He said he never really did anything of real value or importance, but he had taught a Sunday school class once, and he loved and cared for his wife until she died a few years back. He told me he did serve in Korea in the Korean War, and maybe he did one thing while there that made a difference and with that, he began his story:

He said, "I was just a jeep driver in the Army during the Korean war and there was this special day that I was chosen to drive a high-ranking Korean officer around. As we talked the officer asked him about the US Army's chaplaincy program for religious services and education, and he seemed really interested in the idea. The Korean officer, whose name I do not even remember, asked if I could drive him to the headquarters to talk to someone on how US chaplains were appointed and the regulations concerning the program. I took him to various officials that day and out of those encounters, the Korean army started their own chaplaincy corps," and then with a big proud smile he stated, "And I drove the jeep."[17]

Mr. Hagan in his mind was only a simple man, but in reality, he was one of the best and greatest jeep drivers ever. With just a small insignificant gesture he changed the way the Korean Army was established and with a

---

[17] Jeep is a registered trademark by the Fiat/Chrysler Corporation initially trademarked in 1950 by Willys-Overland. In Korea at this time, the US Army used a variety of vehicles all called jeep and manufactured by Ford, and Willys-Overland. Some of the Korea models were left from WWII and were called jeeps or a military code number, G503.

push of the gas and a shift into 3ʳᵈ, he had been a part of God's big plan, for he "drove the jeep."

Which brings me to Joseph in the Christmas story, for he too is often seen as insignificant and unimportant, but he too, "Drove the jeep." He directed Mary and the soon to be born, Baby Jesus, to Bethlehem, and as seen in most pictures of the journey to this "City of David," Joseph is leading a donkey with Mary riding. He is taking his wife to the birthplace of the Savior. He was leading, he was driving the jeep.

"So Joseph also went up from the town in Nazareth in Galilee, to Bethlehem the town of David, because he belonged to the house and line of David." He went there to register with Mary who was pledged to be married to him and was expecting a child." (Luke 2:4-5 NIV).

Remember, like Mr. Hagan and Joseph, you too may feel small and unimportant in the eyes of God, but it is just the opposite. As Mr. Hagan, you may be called to drive the jeep, or like Joseph, to lead the donkey, but God only asks you to be obedient and change the world one gear at a time. So, take the wheel, take the rope, for the donkey is waiting and the jeep is running, for God has great things ahead for you this Christmas. 'Happy "Joseph's Day."

Then Joseph being raised from sleep did as the angel had bidden him, and took unto him his wife: And knew her not till she brought forth her firstborn son: and called his name JESUS.

Matthew 1:24-25. (KJV)

Day Twenty-One
"At Least We Agree on Something"

If you have ever directed the annual, "Christmas" play at your church, you know that it can be one of the most challenging events in your life. There are mothers fighting for their girls to be Mary, while others are asking, "Who will be Joseph and do I have to be a sheep again, and wear that old blanket that looks like a Goodwill reject? Can't we agree that Jason will be a sheep again, and the pastor, a donkey?" (A not too subtle jab). We would try and get the Christmas program off the ground only to be delayed by rain, snow, sleet, or hail. The children will be sick with the winter flu, and the child playing Mary has a broken arm in a cast. The children will be late, the lines of the skit forgotten, and the house robes for shepherds' attire will once again be red and green plaid making them look like Scottish Highlanders. The hats of the Magi will be too big and anything that can go wrong, will.

It is like that first Christmas Day for things were not quite on schedule as well. Mary was pregnant, and Joseph was not the father, and everyone was saying it looked rather "fishy." There was a scandal brewing, and the gossip was thick. It seemed that everything in the marriage started out wrong and everyone in Bethlehem knew it. The pregnancy of Mary was going well, but all the town was talking about how young this Mary was, only 16. It was child abuse, a sexual injunction, and shameful for the family and community. Things were not going well. Joseph was wondering if he had made the right choice in not divorcing Mary and all were puzzled as to what the real truth was.

Joseph had forgotten to make reservations at the Bethlehem Inn that day, and the only place left to stay was in the barn in the back with the sheep, goats, donkeys, and even a camel, and everyone knows how dirty a camel is with all that spitting they do. Then there was the wedding shower and who shows up? Just a bunch of dirty bearded shepherds, who just stared into space and did not enter into any of the wedding games. They were telling some off the wall story of angels and proclamations. It was not going well, and we knew from the start this marriage was going to be a rocky one, you could just tell.

But Mary and Joseph did something right that day that was to infuse their marriage into a rock-solid relationship. They may not have done everything right, but they knew for certain who this baby was and what his name was going to be. You see, an angel had come to Mary and to Joseph, saying the very same thing,

To Joseph the angel said in a dream, "Joseph, son of David, do not be afraid to take Mary home as your wife, because what is conceived in her is from the Holy Spirit. She will give birth to a son, and you are to give him the name, Jesus, because he will save his people from their sins." (Matthew 1:20-21 NIV).

And to Mary, the angel also appeared and stated, "Do not be afraid, Mary, you have found favor with God.

You will be with child and give birth to a son, and you are to give him the name Jesus. (Luke 1:30-31 NIV).

This angel was the first successful marriage and family counselor for at session one of their pre-marital counseling the young couple both agreed to call him, Jesus, which is the Greek form of the name Joshua, meaning, "the Lord saves." They both came to know him as that name implies. Some would say they misnamed the child for he should have been, Joseph, Jr. or something as tradition dictated, but the parents knew he was a "Savior," the one who would save their people from their sins, save us from our imperfections, and save us from ourselves. He even saves us from insignificant and imperfect Christmas pageants.

Even one week later, after all the mishaps and oversites, the young couple is still in agreement, "On the eighth day, when it was time to circumcise him, he was named Jesus…." (Luke 2:21a NIV).

So, this Christmas it doesn't matter if it is the Christmas pageant, or Christmas skit, or Christmas play, it matters that you know who the story is about, and his name is Jesus. At least you can agree on something.

Then Herod, when he saw that he was mocked of the wise men, was exceeding worth, and sent forth, and slew all the children that were in Bethlehem, and in all the coasts thereof from two years old and under according to the time which he had diligently inquired of the wise men.

Matthew 2:16 (KJV)

Day Twenty-Two
"Disappointment"

Christmas is just a couple of days away, right around the corner. It will be here before you know it. You are years away from being ready. There are still gifts to buy and cakes to make, and the house, well it looks like a hurricane stopped in again. You are a little disappointed for the gift you were going to give your son is all sold out, and that cousin you thought would visit at Christmas just called and said he cannot come. You expected him and all year you were looking for his arrival, but I guess maybe he can come next year, but I know it was a disappointment. It really is.

Disappointment, that word, an emotion, a gut feeling that if not checked will lead some to depression and grief, and who wants that at Christmas. You had great expectations, but those expectations were never met, and you are not alone in those feelings.

Disappointed? Of course, but not the same as when the Millerites,[18] a cultic Christian group in the 1800s predicted Christ's second return. In the 1840s, a group called the Millerites were totally filled with

---

[18] Millerites were followers of William Miller, lay Baptist preacher in New York, who after studying the Bible prophecies predicted that Christ would return in 1843-1844.

disappointment for they had predicted Christ would return on October 22, 1844. Many throughout America waited, sat and stared, only to be sorely disappointed as the hours and minutes passed with no change in venue. In fact, when Christ did not come, it went down in history as the day of "Great Disappointment." There were those on that day who by 3:00pm had to be carried off to the hospital laden with heart felt stress and filled with anxiety.

I was not there on that day, but I have been in a society where disappointment is an underlying demon trying the very soul of America. It is not just one day, for it feels like a generation of disappointment. As old hippies, we thought we were going to change the world, when really, we never even changed ourselves. We were filled with expectations of going to Nashville and California and making it big. We wanted to "give peace a chance" but all that was left was running naked at "Burning Man."[19] What a disappointment.

Disappointed? You bet! We even began to teach, "Disappointment Theory" as a new psychological illness so that in therapy we could vocalize our loss and empathize our pain. We displayed our sufferings for all to hear, and still we are disappointed.

But before we go on, the Millerites in the 1840s were on the right path, albeit, slightly misguided. They were looking for Jesus, when in essence he was already here. The Bible tells us that Jesus said, "I have come that you

---

[19] Burning Man is an annual festival in Black Rock City, Nevada to give one experimentation to total self-expression.

might have life, and have it more abundantly." (John 10:10 NIV) and yes, Jesus will come again in the future, but in a few days, we can celebrate his first coming at Christmas and you will not be disappointed.

We wanted to give "peace a chance" as John Lennon[20] sang about expectantly, and yes, there is "Peace on earth, goodwill to men." We wanted to save the world, and yes, Jesus, is the "Lord who saves," for he did come and save us from ourselves, our sin, and our disappointment. We watched expectantly for a change in our culture and in the world in which we live, and on one Christmas Day, God came to earth and began to change the world and it has become a better place ever since. Today, over half the world calls themselves by the name of Christ.

Disappointed that Jesus has not come the 2nd time as foretold? Well, he came once and that has made all the difference. Disappointed that your life is not what you want it to be, then come back to the manger and get a fresh new glimpse of the Christ-child, and know it was not a disappointment, but an appointment in time and space, where even the stars proclaimed his coming, along with angels, shepherds, Wise Men, and the prophets. He came and is still here residing in our hearts and lives. Christmas is just a few days more- expect it.

---

[20] One of the original singers, composer for the group; "The Beatles" who were popular starting in the 1960s.

Day Twenty-Three
"You Will be with Child"

Don't you find it interesting that Luke 1:31(NIV) states that the angel told Mary that she would, "be with child," and it did not say that she would have a baby. I know it is semantics, but I just find it interesting that it is as if the child, the son, already had a persona, an identity, and it was not just a fetal mass or piece of tissue. It suggests from the beginning of the Christmas story that a person would be born that had destiny and a purpose. It was not a chance encounter with a rogue angel, no, this was a child, a man-child, who would change the world. In the Christmas story, the shepherds worshiped Christ as a baby, while a couple of years later, the Magi arrive and bowed down and worshiped the child, which tells me that babies and children, not just adults, are people who are significant and important to all of society.

A while back I was reading a newspaper article in the "Telegraph"[21] about some recent studies on religion and faith. In the article, Dr. Justin Barrett, a senior researcher at the University of Oxford's Centre for Anthropology and Mind, claims that, "young people have a predisposition to believe in a supreme being because they assume that everything in the world was created for a

---

[21] Beckford, M. (2008, November 24). Children are born believers, an academic says. *Daily Telegraph*.

purpose." He went on to say that children must be taught not to believe in God, for children are "born believers."

In a study where six and seven-year olds were asked various questions about life and the nature of the world, they would automatically assume that there was a creator and the creator made the item for a reason. For example, when asked why the first bird was made, they instinctively replied, "So it would make music." They knew that the things that they experienced were made and made for a purpose.

We should not be surprised at this for the Bible tells us that God has shown himself since the beginning of time through his creation and in the things that were made. (Psalms 19, Romans1 KJV). The Bible continues to tell us that his law, his ideas, his very nature is written on our hearts. It is only the fool who says in his heart there is no God. (Psalm 14 KJV).

As adults we need to take lessons from our children for they believe naturally and innocently, longing to pray and desiring to be a part of a God who they are seeking and who is seeking them.

The Bible goes on to say. "…. unless you are converted and become as little children you will by no means enter into the kingdom of heaven." (Matthew 18:3). All through the Bible, references are made to children, and it even calls us, "Children" of God. Therefore, at Christmas, we are not to only worship and bring honor to the babe in swaddling clothes, but also, we are to worship the Christ-child. In essence, we are to become a child in our faith and in our beliefs as well, and worship as a child.

We often think that while we are buying our presents, putting up the Christmas tree, baking the cookies, and shooting the fireworks, that we are doing it all for the children, when in actuality we are doing it so that we too can become like little children and enjoy the season because we too know instinctively that God is real and as his children we are made to worship and adore him. We are made to enjoy Christ.

So, dear children of 2, 12, 22, or 82, come to understand that there is a God, and, in a few days, we will celebrate his birth with anxious hearts, giddy laughter, and thrills of joy, just like a child that you are.

In Rama was there a voice hear, lamentations, and weeping, and great mourning, Rachel weeping for her children, and would not be comforted, because they were not.

But when Herod was dead, behold, an angel of the Lord appeareth in a dream to Joseph in Egypt,

Saying, Arise, and take the young child and his mother, and go into the land of Israel: for they are dead which sought the young child's life.

Matthew 2:18-20 (KJV)

Day Twenty-Four
"Did Christmas Really Happen?"

I tried not to write this book about things trendy and sensational, because life and its journey is new, different, and exciting each and every year. You can never keep current, and this year was new just like all the others. However, every year there is someone who writes another book or an article that supposedly tells the "truth" about Jesus. They will tell you that new documents have been found that will change the face of history and the internet will be filled with new knowledge only known to a few well-read scholars. I remember a few years back when Michael Paulkovich (2016) wrote a book entitled, "Beyond the Crusades."[22] The author stated that he studied over 100 historians and that there was not a single reference outside of the Bible about Jesus. This author, as well as others, stated that they cannot believe in Jesus because all the references about Jesus are from a theological perspective and not historical fact. For Real?

Did they fail to realize that the New Testament is supported by over 24,000 manuscripts that you can touch and feel, with some fragments going back to 50-75 years after the death of Christ. Another fact that they failed to mention is the vast archaeological data that we see that

---

[22] Paulkovich, P. (2016). *Beyond the Crusades: Christianity's Lie, Laws, and Legacy.* Cranford, N.J.: American Atheist Press.

supports time, places, people, and events that happened and were recorded in time and proximity. I lived in the Middle East for years and have walked in the very steps of the Bible. But putting that all aside, let us look at some references to Jesus outside of the Bible, just to put the record straight.

For example, the first century Roman historian, Tacitus, tells us about Pontius Pilate and Jesus and his resurrection and how Christianity spread all over the Middle East and even into Rome. This was confirmed by another Roman, Suetonius, who tells us of the Christian movement and how it caused disturbances all across the Roman Empire. There was also Thallus and Lucian, Pliny the Younger, and Julian Africanus, who all write outside of the church texts and exclaim the existence and nature of Jesus, or the Christ, as some say.

But of course, the famous Jewish historian, Josephus, writes extensively about Jesus and even in text proclaims that "Jesus is the Messiah." Some say he wrote this tongue in cheek, but nevertheless he acknowledges that Jesus was born, was crucified, and rose again from the dead. He may not have been a believer, but he did know his history and wrote of concrete events happening at that time. [23]

We also cannot forget about the vast array of manuscripts and writings of the "Eastern" churches such as the Orthodox, the Nestorians, the Church of the East, and the Coptic Church. We in the West never hear about

---

[23]McDowell, J. (2017). *Evidence That Demands a Verdict*. USA: Thomas Nelson Publishers.

the churches of the Armenians, the Assyrians, and those that exist as far as China. These churches trace their history as far back as the first apostles, such as the Church of St. Thomas, which is still a thriving church in India, having been started by Thomas the apostle prior to his martyrdom.

So, it is Christmas Eve and in the Western tradition, we will celebrate the birth of our Savior tomorrow, and even if you do not believe at least be intellectually honest and proclaim that Jesus did exist; for the shepherds did, the angels did, the Magi did, history did, and all the churches around the world do as well, and you can too.

Christmas Eve is upon us and we are eagerly waiting for the sun to rise on a new Christmas, to be celebrated in all its glory. It is going to be a great day, enjoy it, and enjoy your God, enjoy your church, and enjoy yourself as you come face to face with the fact that Jesus is here.

And he arose, and took the young child and his mother, and came into the land of Israel.
Matthew 2:21 (KJV)

Day Twenty-Five
"Christmas"

Well, we are here, and it has been a long journey, but it is not over yet. We have arrived on the day set aside in the Western tradition for Christmas, and now we celebrate the Christ-child with our family and friends, both young and old, remembering past times and looking forward to even better. It is these moments when memories come flooding in and are awakened once again.

Today, I remember back when I was a young boy and my grandfather was sick and not doing well. He was a poor farmer and he had terminal cancer and as he lay in bed, he too would reminisce about important events in times past, telling me the same stories over and over again. Of course, he would tell you stories that he remembered when he too was young and energetic, and how events unfolded in his life. He had a favorite story he loved to tell about the time when he shot his first squirrel and was able to bring fresh meat home to the family. He would go into great detail about how the squirrel would go around and around the tree, and how he had to outsmart the pesky critter. Then finally he would tell you that with great aptitude on his part, he was able to take aim and with careful precision shoot the fox squirrel and bring it home to Mom for the dinner that night. He would tell that story with great emotion and somewhere in his mind that particular moment was as important as the founding of America on the 4th of July.

But the only problem for me was that if I left the room and returned five minutes later, he would begin to tell the story all over again as if he was telling it for the first time. He repeated himself over and over for he had dementia and when you combined that with the cancer drugs, his intellectual recollection was at times lost. I began to complain to my parents who then related to me that one day I would probably be doing the same thing and I would appreciate someone with a listening ear then as well. And yes, I am slowly approaching the age of my grandfather, and am sad to say, I am doing the same thing. I am telling the same stale jokes and embellish my youth in points unrecognizable. I pray to God that it will stop, but so far it has only gotten worst.

Which leads me to my point on this Christmas Day. I know another person who is very old, really old, and he also keeps repeating himself. He is as old as dirt, in fact, he was here before the dirt was made, and yes, he does repeat himself over and over with the same old stories, but not out of dementia or senility, but out of concern.

He tells us over and over that He loves us, and he gives us the total story of Christmas in just one Bible verse, "For God so loved the world that he gave us his one and only Son…." (John 3:16a NIV). That is what happened today. God gave us himself, in human flesh, so that we too may become one of his children. It is not the Christmas tradition that excites us, but it is the actual giving us of his love in tangible ways that we can know and see, and that means so much more. In fact, he keeps repeating this idea over and over again in hundreds of ways and at various times, as he informs us of his grace and love. He repeats the story in parables and in prophecies. He repeats in from Genesis to Revelation and it sounds like a "broken record," or a "scratched CD," or a robo call that will not stop. But the only thing that is broken is not in the telling, it is in the receiving, for God says this, so that maybe, just maybe, if he says it long enough, and loud enough, and keeps repeating himself, you will get the message and know that it is true. He is wanting you to come this Christmas and lay your burdens down at his feet, and put your head in his arms, and really know, know with no questions asked, that He loves you.

So, let me do as my Grandpa would do and say, "God loves you, and you, and you, and you, and it just doesn't stop. Can I say it again for you know it is Christmas and if you know that he loves you and he came here for you, then you really have something to celebrate and that is, God loves you! And if I have to keep repeating it, so be it, for it will be dementia in its finest hour.

But when he heard that Archelaus did reign in Judaea in the room of his father Herod, he was afraid to go thither: notwithstanding, being warned of God in a dream, he turned aside into the parts of Galilee:

Matthew 2:22 (KJV)

Day Twenty-Six
"Leftovers"

I know the first Christmas in our "38" days of the Christmas journey is over, and we are now running with all our might to the New Year and beyond. However, many of the Christians in the East are still waiting for January 6th or 7th to celebrate Christmas according to the Gregorian calendar, while churches in the West just celebrated Christmas on December 25th according to the Julian calendar. It is not that complicated for whether you celebrate Christ's birth at the end of the year or at the beginning of the next, you will know that He is the Alpha and Omega, the first and the last, and the beginning and the end.

Some of you are already eating leftovers, while others are getting ready for the Christmas feast to come. At our house, we are into the leftovers stage already. There is leftover pie, leftover presents, and maybe even a leftover cousin that I cannot find who is still hanging on, reluctant to leave. Leftover decorations are still up, with a leftover chocolate kiss alone in the bowl, and probably in the back of your fridge, there is a piece of leftover turkey from Thanksgiving as well, waiting to spring forth and give you a sprinkling of salmonella.

Each day we pull out the leftovers and wait for the kids to arrive again so that they can finish off the last vestiges of the holiday season. This year, the apple pie, my favorite is already eaten, but a memory of a past pie once eaten comes to mind.

I had just come home from a late-night visit to one of my parishioners, only to find a piece of an apple pie lingering just for me on the kitchen counter. Not noticing anything unusual, I proceeded to eat the whole piece, downing it with a large glass of milk, only to realize that inside that wonderful morsel, a garden of green fungus was growing. You know the kind I am talking about, the green hairy kind that comes from a late-night murder mystery in which the wife poisons her husband and then runs off to Europe with "Brutus." I hoped it was not the case, but I did keep a watch on my stomach and on my wife, just to make sure she was not planning a long European vacation. But to my relief, all it did was give me an extra shot of penicillin, and my wife only ran off to convenience store for a gallon of milk and to buy me some anti-acids.

But there were some insights that I learned that day that I want to pass on to you. First, just because it looks good on the outside does not mean that all is right on the inside. The package and packaging may look nice, but the gift on the inside may not be what you want. I also learned that green is not my favorite color.

But the most important point that I learned in my pie eating contest is a far more serious question, and that is, "If the pie was poisoned and if I did die, where would I have gone in the afterlife?" I mean Christmas is just over and it was a great time of joy and celebration knowing that God came to earth, but what happens when he calls me to him? In the Bible in Matthew 10:28 (KJV) it tells us not to worry over our body, but to worry over the person inside, our soul.

Again, the Bible warns us, "What good is it for a man to gain the whole world, yet forfeit his soul?" (Mark 8:36 NIV), of if I may paraphrase, "What good is a man if he eats the whole pie and loses his soul in the process.?"

So as to not take away from yesterday's Christmas festivities, let me just remind you today, to look on the inside of yourself, and on the inside of any leftover pie. The pie may not be poisoned but your soul may be, but there is a cure for both, and we know the answer, and his name is Jesus.

But just to clear the air, we can continue this talk over a cup of coffee and a piece of pie, but if you don't mind, I think I will have a donut and a cup of hot tea.

Footnote: I think the pie was a green apple pie. Get it? (I never could tell jokes).

And he came and dwelt in a city called Nazareth: that it might be fulfilled which was spoken by the prophets, He shall be called a Nazarene.

Matthew 2:21 (KJV)

Day Twenty-Seven
"It's a Circus Out There"

The week after Christmas is one of the strangest weeks of the year, having been crammed between Christmas and New Year's, you really don't know if Christmas is over or the New Year has come. You go to work, kind of, and you are off from work, kind of, and family is around, kind of, and the week really gets hectic. You begin to take the broken toys back to the store, and you go and exchange ill-fitting shoes, and the batteries are out of juice, leftovers are in the fridge, and ….

I went to the store and it was a "circus" with everyone running around in a mad rush to nowhere. For me it started with a daughter-in-law being deathly sick with a pregnancy, an accident with a hit and run driver, a fire at my building, a move by my son, and a sound system that did not work again at the church. That was the first day. I told my wife that I am going to sit, do nothing, and see what happens next.

It reminded me of a scripture in Amos 5:19(NIV), "It will be as though a man fled from a lion only to meet a bear, as though he entered his house and rested his hand on the wall, only to have a snake bite him." You too have been there and some of you are saying now, "You're right about that one for that is the way my week is going too." It went from bad to worst and then when I did finally get home, out of the rat race and the circus of life, a snake came and bit me. What a week!

That "lion" of a boss sent a new directive opposite of the one you received yesterday, and it contradicts all that he said in a staff meeting the week before.

I just got my car out of the repair shop and that "snake" of a neighbor that I confronted last week "keyed" my car and of course, my insurance does not cover vandalism.

My spouse came home angry with a "beast" of an attitude and was upset because a co-worker walked off the job.

I lost my cell phone for the third time in a day, and I have a "bear" of a cough, and I sat down to rest in my easy chair only to sit on my glasses and break them.

It was bears, lions, and snakes running everywhere, and I thought the circus had left town.

But be encouraged, look up, for the Bible tells us that the lion will be tamed, and will eat straw like an ox. It reminds me too that we will tread on serpents and snakes, and it continues to let us know that, "The infant will play near the hole of the cobra and the young child will put his hand into the viper's nest. They will neither harm or destroy on my holy mountain, for the earth will be full of the knowledge of the Lord as the waters cover the sea." (Isaiah 11: 8-9 NIV). All will be okay.

The Bible tells us that one day the huge "beast" that threatens to devour us and our world will be destroyed, and "He will wipe every tear from their eyes." (Revelation 21:4 NIV).

So, this week, this crazy week between the holidays, remember the circus is leaving town and is taking most of his creatures with him, for there is a better show in town, down at the Nativity Display in front of the church where, "the cattle are lowing, and the baby awakes, but probably heard that song before, and it's a good one, much better than the circus barker and his message. So, sing God's song and you might even want to join Barry McGuire, that old original "Jesus Freak" as he sings on this journey of discovery: "Now it's a happy road that we're traveling on, I just can't help myself, He has me singing a happy, happy song."[24]

In the beginning was the Word, and the Word was with God, and the Word was God.

The same was in the beginning with God.

John 1:1-2 (KJV)

[24] McGuire, B. (1975). *Happy Road* (Song). Brentwood, Tenn., Sparrow Records

Day Twenty-Eight
"The God Who Sees You"

As you know, in the first few months after Christmas we see more suicides, more fatalities, and more deaths than usual. I am not sure why, but I suspect it has to do with loss and grief over past dreams abandoned, or maybe the loss of a spouse, a child, or a friend, and the memory lingers. For some, Christmas, instead of a joyous time, is a time of extreme loneliness, like being in the middle of a crowd and no one knows you. We find that scenario in the Bible when David wrote in Psalm 55:6 (NIV), "I said, Oh that I had the wings of a dove! I would fly away and be at rest- I would flee far away and stay in the desert." We just want to get away from it all, just like David did, and I have done just that very thing.

At various times of anguish and hardship, we wish that we could just vanish into the night, sight unseen, and hide where nobody knows us. We could build us a cabin at Wolf Creek and live the life of a virtual, "Daniel Boone." We would be at peace, for no one really cares and no one really knows that we exist. It would just be me, alone, enjoying the solitude of oneness with one's self. It is a dream that every 10-year-old boy builds in his mind when Dad and Mom are on his back. We will just run away.

But there is an interesting story in the Bible about a person who did just that. In Genesis 16, Hagar, the slave girl is pregnant by her master Abram and she is the second wife, the outsider, and is cast out of the family and into the desert. She runs away and is in the plight of many a young lady, who find themselves in a situation that looks hopeless, and in a place strange and far away from home. She is all alone sitting next to a spring in the desert, and in need of someone who would help, and someone who would understand. But while sitting there someone does come, for an angel of the Lord came, and told her things about her life, about her future, and about her son to come. She came to the knowledge that there was a God, a God who saw her in her present condition and cared. She gave a name to this Lord of her life, the one who spoke to her on that day, and she called him, "You are the God who sees me," for she said, "I have now seen the One who sees me." (Genesis 16:13b NIV).

We sometimes feel that God only watches us to catch us doing sinful things, and then to punish us, but really God is watching us and is ready to show us he cares. As Hagar in her troubles, God wants you to know that he sees you. He sees your best friend has died. He sees that you can't kick that drug habit. He sees that you are pregnant, and the father has left you alone. He is the God who sees, "you."

But you also see that Hagar took a step toward God, for she states that, "I have now seen the One who sees me." It is the same in the Christmas story as well. Remember in the Christmas story in Luke where it says, "When they (shepherds) had seen him, they spread the word concerning what had been told them about this child, and all were amazed at what the shepherds said to them." (Luke 2:17-18 NIV).

You must understand that there is a seeing and being seen, for God sees and we see God, and then we listen as Hagar did and as the Shepherds did and people are amazed at the story we tell. There is this communication, a conversation, a real dialog between you and God, a God who wants to see you.

You may have felt that you are lost in the desert of life, but you are not, you are not alone, and you are not unknown. God knows, and God sees and aren't you thankful he does.

All things were made by him: and without him was not anything made that was made.

In him was life; and the life was the light of men.

John 1:3-4 (KJV)

Day Twenty-Nine
"Too Much of a Good Thing"

Too much of a good thing, you bet there is. A few years back we were on the road heading to my sister's house for Christmas and we were singing, "I'm Dreaming of a White Christmas,"[25] and being from South Texas, most of the time that is just a dream. But as we made our way north, the snow kept coming and coming and before you know it, we had our "White Christmas" and more, so much more. It was too much of a good thing.

But today they are always telling us the same story over and over again as well, "You ate too much at Thanksgiving and you had better be careful this Christmas. You may just have too much of a good thing." Too much sun is bad for your skin. Too much candy is bad for your sugar level. Too much fat is not good for your cholesterol. Too much water every night in the bathtub is bad for your electric bill. (I will hear about this one from my wife as she goes swimming every night in the tub, and in the deep end,)

Too much of a good thing is not good and too much of a bad thing is even worst. As a pastor, I think that too much "religion" may not be a good thing and something to be avoided. It is like an aunt I had who

---

25 Berlin, I. (1942), *White Christmas* (Song). Los Angeles, Decca Records.

loved, "religion" so much that she went to church twice on Sundays, once on Wednesday nights for Bible Study, Tuesdays for ladies' Discovery Class, Fridays for all night prayer, and Saturdays at least once a month for "Pancakes and Prayer", however she never had time to go fishing with her husband or to the movies with her children. She had too much of religion, but not enough of Jesus.

But the Bible does tell us to have some things in excess and to be filled to overflowing. We are to be filled with care, filled with the Holy Spirit, filled with joy, and filled with righteous (Philippians 1:9 KJV). It goes on to tell us be filled and overflowing with thanksgiving, with love for each other, and with love for our Lord. However, to understand this fully, you must be aware that since no one can look inside your heart, the only way people can tell if you are filled is, if you are overflowing and they see the overflow.

At Christmas you have noticed everything is over the top, with angels singing, dreams foretold, people in amazement, stars in new places, and prophecies fulfilled. It was a once in a lifetime experience.

But we are past the 25th of December Christmas Day and we are into the time of the baby Jesus' dedication and circumcision in the Temple. We are past the too much snow phase, but it just keeps on coming. Simeon has been waiting in the Temple courts for all of his life to see the Lord's Christ and there he was, right in Simeon's arms- it was way over the top, overflowing, it was too much snow. Simeon was holding God in his arms- now if that is not too much, then nothing is too much. Then following that, another servant of God, a widow of 84 years, Anna, experienced the same thing, and it was too much snow, and the snow kept coming. (Luke 2 KJV)

The Bible in John says it this way, "The Word became flesh and made his dwelling among us. We have seen his glory, the glory of the One and Only, who came from the Father full of grace and truth." (John 1:14 NIV).

Jesus was not just full of grace and truth, it overflowed, the snow was a blizzard, a monster of a storm.

Too much snow? You know it. Too much religion? It has to be true. But too much of Jesus and his love, well you cannot get enough, and it needs to overflow. Too much of a good thing? No way! It just keeps getting better and better, so sing along with me, "Let it Snow, Let it Snow, Let it Snow," and declare like Paul, the apostle, as he blesses his friends with, "May the Lord make your love increase and overflow for each other and for everyone else, just as ours does for you." (I Thessalonians 3:12 NIV).

And the light shineth in darkness; and darkness comprehended it not.

John 1:5 (KJV)

Day Thirty
"Games People Play"

The week is almost over as we rush towards the New Year just days ahead. If your family is like mine, we have brought out the board games this week and have been playing them much of the time. I do not know what kind of game your family likes to play whether it is Scrabble or The Settlers of Katan, but for years we always had the Christmas Monopoly Marathon.[26]

This morning I have just landed on Boardwalk and my son wants his rent money now. I am only left with Baltic Avenue and this game of Monopoly has come to another cruel heartless end as once again he takes all my money and leave me penniless. My son is a tyrant, a land grabbing shyster, an uncompromising member of the Mafia, (If I offended any mafia member, I am sorry), a sadistic savage, a…. you get the picture. He plays to win, and he doesn't cheat, but by the end of the game, everybody is angry with him. He is sitting at the board with his filthy cash flowing from his pockets, rich, but with the family vowing never to play Monopoly with him again. A tyrant I say. And then my wife pops up, "Honey, it is just a game."

But life is not just a game, which brings me to my point. Life is not just a game to be played, a game of chance, a roll of the dice, where if you get Boardwalk and

---

[26] Board games popular with children and adults

Park Place you win. You think that if you just win the Lottery, you will be happy. You go from one game to another, always thinking that you will win, when in reality you have never won anything of value in you search for the key to happiness. You think if I can roll sevens just one more time, or land on the right square, then tonight I will take home the $69.70 in the Bingo pot and be forever rich.

But let me remind you of what Einstein once said, "God does not play dice," which validates the idea that life is more than a game of chance and that the universe and you were created for a reason. God says he knew you from your mother's womb (Psalm 139 NIV) and that he knows your very name as we read earlier in one of our 38 days' discussions. You were not a mistake, you were not the result of a one-night stand, "No," you are a child of God made in his image to bring joy to your heavenly Father by an act of your will to serve him and love him because he first loved you. (I John 4:19 NIV).

Yes, you want to win, and you will, but on God's terms. It reminds me of the time when I had a debate with a Marine Colonel in church on being a "pacifist." To me it appeared that I had won the debate, but years later, the only thing that my opposing friend remembered was not my win but my arrogance and determination just to win, to be right. I had won the fight, but I had lost the war. I came across sadistic and haughty, and with my ego in place I joined the ranks of the Sadducees and Pharisees.[27]

And sometimes at Christmas we come across with our slogans, "Keep Christ in Christmas," and "Wise Men Still Follow Him," not realizing that we are saying we are wise and pious, and they are not. We must understand if the gospel is good news then it is good news to everyone.

The "good news" is that Christmas is not where winners gather to exchange stories of extravagant gifts and how they won out this year; no, it where losers proclaim the good news of losing: Losing sin, losing pride, and losing the battle. I do not know about you, but I am tired of trying to always be first, to be number one, to be on top. I am ready to let Christ win this Christmas.

And besides, Baltic is not much to look at and who really wants Boardwalk anyway? Can we begin to play another game, how about the Azores game.... where did all my family just go? Everyone, really, it's a fun game. It's my oldest son and daughter-in-law's favorite game of all time.

There was a man sent from God, whose name was John.
John 1:6 (KJV)

---

[27] Sadducees and Pharisees were the keepers and judges of the Jewish law in the time of Christ.

Day Thirty-One
"New Year's Eve"

Tonight, is one of those nights that I just cannot stand to celebrate. New Year's parties are all the rage and the office parties of unbridled emotions and drink is not something that actually inspires me. You may call me an old geezer and I probably am, but I am sorry but what happens on New Years' night usually has consequences that are just not worth it.

I know this not from a New Year's event, but from an event that sticks in my mind to this day. Let me tell you the story. Years back, when I was a young man, a little boy to be exact, the smallest in my class, I got into some situations just a little out of hand, literally. In Louisiana, the highway in front of our house was being widened into a four-lane road, and they were taking our house place, but instead of moving out we just moved our house back away from the road. During the move we had to make certain considerations, and one of them was to use an old outhouse left years ago in times of want. It was an ancient structure, sided with black tarpaper and a wooden throne, with a smell that let you know that this was the area of last resort. It was awful, did I say awful? Really!

At the time, I was the younger brother and still am to be sure, five years younger to be exact, and my brother could talk me into anything. On this particular day, my wiser older brother discovered two Coke[28] bottles lying inside of the outhouse pit. He came up with a brilliant strategy for extracting these treasures for they were worth five cents deposit apiece, which would buy each of us a piece of candy at Stevens Store. He suggested that I climb down through the hole and into this cavern of dung, and he would hold my legs as I descended. With granddaddy long-legged spiders crawling on my hands and spider webs covering my face, I began my descent, and descent it was, for my brother lost his grip and down I went. I still get night sweats just thinking of this horrific event. As I said, some things are just not worth it. I came to understand that the rewards gained are not worth the price paid.

It is like tonight when the devil beguiles you with wanton lust and unbridled greed as he suggests you too descend into the pit. He promises you that he will catch you, he will hold you, and he will be there, but he drops you on your face into a declining, unsavory world of man and beast. He tells you that the rewards will be candy sweet, and that you will come out smelling like a rose, but take it from a kid who knows, the pit is not where roses grow.

There is a lesson in the world of humankind that only God can teach and tell you, and the lesson is this, God will, "Lift you out of the slimy pit, out of the mud and mire; he set my feet on a rock and gave me a firm

---

[28] Coke is a name used in the Southern part of America to mean any brand of soft drink, but it is a registered trademark of the Coca-Cola Co.

place to stand. He put a new song in my mouth, a hymn of praise to our God." (Psalm 40:2-3 NIV).

He will even lift you out of a ten-cent cavity of despair, even if your brother won't. Some gifts are free, but others way too costly, and as I said, "It is just not worth it." So, this New Years' get out another board game, "Life," and play it and win.

P.S. By the way , I did get the Coke bottles and cashed them in for the deposit and remember that time when you drove through Louisiana on that hot summer day and got a cold soft drink for you and your wife, look again it may have been those very bottles.

The same came as a witness, to bear witness of the Light, that all men through him might believe.

John 1:7 (KJV)

Day Thirty-Two and Day One
"Happy New Year"

We have just passed a major marker on our "38" days of Christmas journey, for we have started a New Year and are racing towards our second Christmas celebration that we will enter into celebration with our churches and brothers and sisters of the East. By now, you may have made some New Year's resolutions, but of course, you broke last years, so why even try. I mean why bother when you did not get it right the first time.

I was talking to a friend tonight and we were asking ourselves the same question, "When do you get it together?" When does the world smooth out and you get to coast for a while. When do you get to ride your bicycle again, feet upon the handlebars, with wind blowing in your face? When do we get to play Pac-Man[29] again and laugh out loud as you skunk your opponent? It seems all through our lives, we start, but there is just one thing missing, one extra game to play, one more chess move to make to call checkmate, as we chase that elusive butterfly with hands just inches away.

We begin but we get it wrong and we need a second chance, and we need to start over one more time. We have learned that we cannot be trusted to get it right, and last year was no exception. We failed again miserably, and

---

[29] Pac-Man was a video game that was popular and appeared in 1980 when video games were first coming out.

we know it. Again, I say, I need a second chance, another try, another real effort to make it go the way it should.

And you have it…...

Lighting was flashing, and the fog was just lifting as Moses made his way down the mountain, holding in his hands with extreme agility the most important revelation of God to man. In his hands were the tablets containing the commandments, the laws of God, what we now call the 10 Commandments, written by God's very hand. It was the most valuable of manuscripts, ones that were to be God's laws given to man: "You should not steal, You should have no Gods before me…." And the list went on.

But something terrible happened, for as Moses returned and saw the people in the camp languishing in revelry and lust, he threw the stone tablets to the ground in anger, breaking then into tiny pieces of religious insignificance. It a moment, in an emotional outburst, Moses forever changed his relationship with his God. He had taken the sacred and made it profane. It appeared to be over, finished, for this had been, as some would say, "A total lack of judgement."

Moses, however, finds his place in the, "Tent of Meeting," the place where God sends his presence and there God speaks to Moses and says, "Chisel out two stone tablets like the first ones, and I will write on them the words that were on the first tablets, which you broke." (Exodus 34:1 NIV).

In essence, God gave Moses a "2nd Chance."

So, you made a mess of last year, and events did not go as planned. You did have a lack of judgement when you left your wife and children. You did have a lack of judgement when you left your job and cursed your boss as you went out the door. You broke it, you made a mess out of God's laws and you left the work of God in a thousand pieces at your feet. It seemed it could not be fixed, but it can, for God reaches down to you and says, "Let's start over again." You really goofed the first time, but we will chisel out the tablets just like before.

You see, you can never get it right. This lack is an "Act of God," for it causes you to always have to rely on him, therefore you can never be self-sufficient. He created that insufficiency in you so that you will know you can trust only in God. The Bible tells us to, "Trust in God with all your heart and lean not on your own understanding.... (Proverbs 3:5 NIV).

This year, like Moses, come to understand that God is the God of the 2nd chance, and the 3rd, and he loves you with an everlasting love. Start the year with God and He, not you, will see it through.

He was not that Light, but was sent to bear witness of that Light.

John 1:8 (KJV)

Day Thirty-Three
"Jesus, Only Jesus"

You probably have noticed by now that we have not touched on most of the other Christmas stories. We have not talked about the Legend of the Candy Cane, or the History of the Christmas Tree, or even the Origin of the True Santa Claus, in essence, these stories seem so minor when placed beside the actual Christmas Story. Which leads me to a really weird story, a personal one.

The other night I had a really weird dream and I am not making this up. It was not a typical pizza dream after eating the whole thing, but it was very unusual, so let me explain. In my dream, I was with a friend and we had been asked to speak at his huge church without a name, but upon arrival at the church I suddenly realized that I did not have a Bible, or any notes, or a message, or anything. I only had a water pistol that squirted out scriptures (I told you it was weird). My glasses were cracked, and I had one lens missing. I did not know what to say and so I just stood there for quite some time and then I said, "All I can tell you about is Jesus." And that was it. It was at this time that I awoke and, in a half, dazed sleep I began to ponder what it all meant. I am not a

C.S. Lewis[30] and my fantasy quotient is very small, but I decided that maybe, just maybe, this dream had a point.

So, this is what I came up with....

When I really get to the main point in life, it is always about Jesus and nothing more. Jesus said this in the Bible over and over, and like a never-ending story the end is always the same. In the Bible it admonishes us to feed the poor and take care of the hungry, and we see that Jesus did just that with the feeding of the 5000, and then he tells the crowd, "I am the bread of life."

When the blind man, who cannot find his way back home, comes to Jesus needing Jesus' healing touch, he goes home healed with the message from Jesus saying, "I am the door."

When Lazarus is dead, and the family is asking Jesus to bring him back to life, Jesus replies, "I am the resurrection and the life."

When a prostitute has been caught plying her trade all night and is caught in the web of darkness, and then brought to Jesus for him to judge, he replies, "I am the light of the world."

When the disciples are confused in their leadership abilities and cannot find peace of mind, Jesus tells them, "I am the good shepherd."

---

[30] CS Lewis was a theologian, writer, and philosopher that is considered by many to be the foremost theologian/thinker of the 20th century.

Jesus appears to be saying, "If you need healing, I am it. If you need food for the asking, I am it. If you need direction, I am it. If you need life, I am it. In fact, what he is saying is that whatever you need, I am it."

He is saying, "Don't seek the healing, seek the healer. Don't seek food handouts, seek the bread of life. Don't seek comfort, seek the comforter. Don't seek wisdom, seek the wisdom giver." We are spending all of our time on the issues and their outcomes, when we need to spend our time with the one who decides what the outcome is. The one who says, "I am…." And nothing more.

So, in these next few days of the Christmas season, let us not seek to know about Christmas, let us seek to know about Christ, and if we do, we will need nothing more.

That was the true Light which lightest every man that cometh into the world.

John 1:9 (KJV)

Day Thirty-Four
"Saving Ebola"

Today I am sitting at my desk going through my mail and getting ready to throw most of it the garbage. It is from various charities that made Christmas appeals to get your money so that you could get tax write offs before the end of the year. They are really quite funny for many of them have nothing at all to do with Christmas, unless as previous told, manatees were part of the manger, and Herod is the poster child for the charity, "Negative Population Growth." There are charities for the conservation of the rain forest, the deserts, the mountains, the oceans, space, the moon, and even clean air. I tried to help on the last one for clean air and held my breath for a minute, but to no avail. It wasn't clean anyway unless you are from Italy, for I had eaten a garlic laden pizza and my breath polluted the air in spite of my best efforts.

But as you can see, there are charities for everything, from smoking prevention to marijuana enhancement. There are charities for the sick, the lame, the well, the tall, and the short. There are charities for every kind of person on earth. I am looking at Iranian charities asking you for money so that they can eliminate Jewish charities, and Costa Rican watermelon farmers are asking for money so that they can get an upper hand on those coffee growers from Columbia. There is the "Bread of the World" letter next to the "Gluten-Free Fellowship."

And then there are the wildlife charities with their cries to, "Save the Whales, Save the Monkeys, Save the Panda Bears and the one I like, "The Ruffled Grouse Society." We are saving everything from trout, to wolves, and even to "Dogs on Death Row." There are the organizations, quite comical, like "Puppies Behind Bars," along with "Puppies Who go to Bars."

There seems to be no end to names and causes, but there were a few animals that were missing. I noticed that we like the big animals and the ones that are cute and cuddly, but how about the little guys? I mean, how about those microorganisms, such as the lonely bacteria, and others who have been given a bad rap such as, "Ebola"[31] and the "Polio Virus."[32] We have almost eliminated them and what a horror that would be if they too become extinct. Just because they are little and have caused a few problems doesn't mean that they are not important too. I mean every dog or cat needs to be house broken, don't they, and we don't kill them if they have a little accident on the carpet.

But I hope you see now, that I say this all-in jest, but to get to the point; there are some invisible things that really do need saving this year. I am speaking of your soul. It is there, and you know it, you feel it speaking to you. You need to save that inner man, that spiritual man from the horrors of sin and misuse. Although it may appear to

---

[31] Ebola is a disease-causing virus that is rampant in the continent of Africa.

[32] Polio was a crippling disease at the turn of the century and was almost eradicated by the 1950s in America.

be insignificant now, one day it will be the only thing that matters. It will be the only part of you that lives on, and so you need to save it, and in that case, you need a Savior. You may have missed the discussion on the December 25th Celebration of Christmas, but you have another chance to make your soul right as you meet the, "Lord who Saves," Jesus.

You can join his charity, his charity of love called, "Save Your Soul Today." Jesus has a self-addressed stamped envelope where you can send you sins to him, your life to him, and he will save you from extinction, and you will live on from now to eternity.

"Save Ebola" well, not today, but the "Save Souls" charity, that makes more sense, so, yes, I think I will give to that charity and I still have time to do so before Christmas, the Christmas celebrated in January by our family members who are in the churches throughout the Eastern world, to whom we say, first Happy New Years and then a Merry Christmas.

He was in the world, and the world was made by him, and the world knew him not.

John 1:10 (KJV)

Day Thirty-Five
"Communicating Christ and Christmas"

Some of you when you started this "38" Day Christmas Journey, had no idea of the vastness of the church and who we are as churches, both East and West. So, after looking at the Christmas of December 25th, we are going to turn and celebrate the Christmas of January 7th. Each church carries on their various Christmas traditions, with some ancient rites dating to the era of the apostles. The Christian church was initially established in the city of Antioch on the Orontes River, which is the present city of Antakya, Turkey. While Turkey is a country where East and West meet, this city is firmly in the Middle East. It was here that the believers in Christ were first called, "Christians." (Acts 11:25 NIV). But as you can see it was not Rome, nor Istanbul (Constantinople), or anywhere else in the West where the church had its beginning, it was in the East and it was from here where Paul was sent out on his first missionary journey and the church began to flourish. The church grew and multiplied and went in all directions with the disciples going as far as India and maybe even to China to the East, Ethiopia to the South, Russia to the North, and Europe to the West. And it is from all the churches that we learn how to live and be called Christians.

Therefore, having lived most of my ministerial life in the Middle East and Japan, I found that I had to listen more and say less as I endeavored to communicate Christ and of course, Christmas. I remember when I first went to a country in the Far East and talked about how Christ came at Christmas and later died and shed his blood and that too is a celebration of what is now called the Lord's Supper, the native countrymen remarked that I came across like a cannibal feasting on the body of those long dead. I used the religious vocabulary of which I was familiar, but it came across in ways I never thought.

It was the same in Albania and Turkey as well, for we are pastors would give out our humanitarian aid, bringing in doctors and nurses, professors, businessmen, and even beauticians, and then wonder what we communicated about Jesus through these efforts. As we gave away cosmetics that were donated, did we communicate to the ladies in our churches that Jesus loves only pretty women that are physically fit, intelligent, with pockets full of money. I hope not.

I even tried to use object lessons bringing in a jar of ants and explained how if I was to really communicate to these ants in the jar, I would have to use ant language and become an ant. I thought that would easily communicate the Christmas message of "Christ coming to earth," only to have my listeners hear me say that Christ was a reincarnated ant.

So, I thought I needed to listen to the Church of the East, one that I did not know much about and hear what they said and how they communicated Christ. I needed to hear from them and learn how to think differently, not that my thinking was bad, it was just not thinking the way they thought.

It really came home to me at one Bible study where I was trying to explain to a group of Iranian refugees the Bible verse, Mark 9:43 (NIV), where it states, "If you hand causes you to sin, cut if off. It is better for you to enter life maimed then with two hands go into hell." Now that is a hard verse to explain, but then one of my Iranian friends said, I understand that verse completely, for you see in Iran if you are caught stealing, a sin, a crime, then someone can cut your hand off for the crime that was committed, but this verse says, if your hand causes you to sin, then you must cut it off. It means that you must take care of the sin yourself and not wait until you get caught by God or by someone else and they have to cut it off; cut the sin out yourself.

It was the best explanation of that verse and got me off the hook for not knowing what to say. So, what I am endeavoring to say is that Jesus is not some hipster in skinny jeans and a plaid shirt, playing rearranged Beatle songs on his new Stratocaster, nor is he a cultural icon of the West with a smiling face and a trimmed beard. It manners not that we celebrate on the 25th or on the 7th, Jesus is still that "Babe in a Manger" coming as God to man, saving us from our sin and self, and taking us one day to be with him again in heaven, and that is the message of Christmas, plain and simple, with no cutesy lines or funny illustrations, bridging both East and West for all mankind to see.

He came unto his own, and his own received him not.

John 1:11 (KJV)

Day Thirty-Six
"Christmas and Culture"

We are still on our journey and almost to the end, and we have explored the Christmas Story from the perspective of the Shepherds, the Angels, Mary and Joseph, and even the donkey. We have tried to examine Christmas in cultural terms and in historical facts, and even looked into a couple of funny stories to drive home a point, but today, put on your thinking caps and join with me in exploring Christmas from Christ's perspective as that babe, that child, that has just been born.

Christ was born as the ultimate cultural challenge for social workers international. He was the extreme 3rd culture kid and I am sure it was quite an adjustment for him personally as you see him having to go from time to time to speak to God the Father and readjust his thinking. He would go off to the mountain and pray and come back renewed.

So, who are these 3rd culture kids? They are called many things today: immigrant children, military brats, missionary kids (MKs), and foster children to name a few. It means any of those children who, because of their parents' occupation or ethnicity, move a lot, speak a different language or two, and feel misplaced due to barriers seen and unseen.

For example, military children know that they will live in one place a few years only to be transferred across the globe because of a new assignment, just when they are beginning to make friends. Immigrant children try to straddle two cultures, two languages, two sets of traditions, moving from side to side just trying to fit in. It is hard on these children for sure.

These 3rd culture children have a strenuous time in putting down roots and making friendships. They commit themselves to their friends, but not really, for they give only a small portion of their heart to their companions, for they know soon they will leave and start it all over again. They make friends superficially and leave true friendships only for family.

I have been there too being a military brat and a pastor overseas and I have left many friends as well, Bato in Albania, Ercan in Cyprus, and many more. Some of you feel as disjointed as I do and as Christians, we all do, for we are all 3rd culture children; we are in this world and the culture that surrounds it, but we are in another world too, waiting to make the move.

As Jesus we start asking questions of those around us, just like Jesus did, for we know Jesus was the ultimate missionary kid having left heaven to come to earth, knowing that in 33 years he would be leaving family and friends. He asked his disciples, Do you want to leave too, do you? (John 6:67 NIV), as he sought to maintain their friendships. He was feeling that loss that comes with the move that was to be a permanent one. He even wanted to insure them and himself as he told his disciples that he no longer called them slaves or servants, he called them friends. (John 15:15 NIV).

But there is good news for all you 3rd culture Christians: Jesus never left. He remains your friend, my friend, for he said, "I will never leave you nor forsake you." (Hebrews 13:5 KJV). He came at Christmas and has left for a short time, but you can still talk to him, pray to him, and commune with him 24/7, and one day in the future Jesus will come back physically for all to see.

We have a God that understands completely what MKs feel, how military kids survive, what foster children experience, and how children from other countries live in a new culture with a new language. Jesus knows, for he has been there too.

So, this Christmas, look at that Christ-child a little more closely, wipe those tears from your eyes, take that frown off your face, and give your whole heart to the one who gave his whole heart and life to you. You may live in the East or the West, but it is the same Jesus that loves us all. Our second Christmas is almost here, and we can celebrate again with all our friends.

But as many as received him, to them gave he power to become the sons of God, even to them that believe on his name:

John 1:12 (KJV)

Day Thirty-Seven
"Utopia"

If you started on day one, you have almost reached your destination in the "38" days of Christmas for now it is Christmas Eve again and we are waiting for the Christ-child. You started, and you began to head in a certain direction, not knowing what you would find, but nevertheless you knew you were on the road to Christmas. You may have been running away, but now you are running to someplace, somewhere, and to someone. You are no longer like the man who was buying a ticket from the train conductor, who when asked where he was going and what ticket he needed, the man replied, "If you don't know where you are going, anywhere will do, just give me a ticket to somewhere."

Many of us started this trip seeking a place of perfection, a place of safety and solitude, a place where you could call home. You were looking for what Americans say is the beacon on the hill, that place above all others, the home where only happiness and peace prevail, that "utopia' of impeccable excellence. It will be that place that mankind has sought for all ages, but now we may really be able to find it: a utopia for all men and women, of all races, of all languages and cultures, and of all classes.

"Utopia" was first mentioned by Sir Thomas Moore[33] in 1516 in a novel where a fictional society was born on an island in the Atlantic, where a union of men and women co-existed in complete harmony and governance. It came as an idea sought but never found.

Many in America have tried to make such a society. There was Rugby, Tennessee, and Ephrata, Pennsylvania, and one I knew well, New Llano, Louisiana. Our family once owned the headquarters building of the New Llano Colony only to see it burnt to the ground after the grand society had followed suit. Nirvana ceased to exist, and the grand experiment failed to produce the lasting effects.

But there are other "topias" that exist as well. There is the "eutopia," which is a perfect society, and "dystopia or outopia" which is an unrealistic society of perfection.

Once in America, we wrote in the Preamble of the Constitution, that we desired to make a "more perfect union" a eutopia, only to find we had created a utopia, a _fictional_ place of perfection. In fact, how could you have a "more perfect union," which is a contradiction in terms, for if something is perfect, nothing more can be added or needed.

But something more is needed for we know that perfection cannot rise out of imperfection. We cannot change a letter or two, a phrase or a sentence, or political party, and expect life to change overnight. No, we must start with perfection to have perfection, and since I have not met a perfect person, man cannot make heaven on earth. Heaven can only start in heaven, and only when

---

[33] Moore, T. (1516). *Utopia*. Netherlands.

heaven touches earth does perfection prevail. There must be a start, a beginning in perfection, and that is exactly what we find in the Bible, for it begins in Genesis 1 (NIV) with, "In the beginning God..." and that is where we must begin. That is where we take the first step. That is the beginning of all things created and without God, it matters not if it is East or West, it will only be a "Utopia," which by definition is an unrealistic view of mankind. There are no Tibetan sanctuaries, no native sweat lodges, no monastic retreat centers that can produce lasting perfection in mankind, but there is a perfect God that by his grace and his coming to man at Christmas can produce a "more perfect union;" a union of God and man, based on a sinless God forgiving a sinful man.

In Galatians 4:4-6 (NIV), it reads as this, "But when the time had fully come, God sent his Son, born of a woman, born under the law, to redeem those under the law that we might receive the full rights of sons. Because you are sons, God sent the Spirit of his Son into our hearts, the Spirit who call out, 'Abba,' Father.

And that time has come, for in just a few hours, we will celebrate Christmas again with all the sons and daughters of God, both East and West, who are our sisters and brothers in Christ, for we all share the same God, the one Father. I am excited, how about you? I bet you are too.

Which were born, not of blood, nor of the will of the flesh, nor of the will of man, but of God.

John 1:13 (KJV)

Day Thirty-Eight
"Christmas Again"

It's Christmas Day again, all over, for the 2nd time and you get to enjoy the festivities with church bells ringing, carols singing, pastor preaching, and the Christmas liturgy being said all over again. It is an honored privilege to join with our colleagues in the Eastern Churches today and wish them all a very, "Merry Christmas." I hope you enjoyed the Christmas journey along with me and I hope you experienced a little more of the Christmas Season than you did from the year before. I pray that nothing of Christmas' greatness and God's glory was lost in the busyness of this time of year.

However, for some people Christmas does cause one to remember both the good and the bad, as with the loss of a loved one or the loss of past activities that kindled a real joy with family and friends. I was talking to an old pastor friend of 96 years of age, and at various holiday events I would find him alone, for his wife of many years had passed on a few years back. This time in my consolation, I came up to him and lovingly said, "Pastor Robinson, I am so sorry for the loss of your wife," trying to show compassion for her demise, to which he stopped me in mid-sentence and replied, "Lost? I know exactly where she is," and then proceeded to give me a mild rebuke for not remembering that he was assured to see her again in eternity. Yes, Christmas again.

Lost, yes things have gotten lost at times, which reminds me of a time when I lost something special for me as a young 6-year-old boy. I had a large collie dog, that kind of dog that you remember with fondness and reminisce over. We called him, "Boy," because we always said, "Here boy, Here boy," and he would come running, so his name had to be, "Boy." Plus, he was of the male gender, so what other name would you use? In fact, we've named every other collie we've had since then the same name. Original, yeh?

But one day we had gone over to the neighbors' house with Boy, went inside, and told Boy to stay on the front porch as we joined our friends inside for fun and play. Leaving that evening to return home, we exited the back door, absent-mindedly forgetting to take our dog who was on the front porch home with us.

Waking the next morning, we ran outside expecting to be greeted by that wagging tail and collie breath, only to realize Boy was nowhere to be found. We called. We looked, and we searched everywhere. He was lost. We had lost our dog. He was nowhere to be found. That is, until we retraced our steps and found Boy still waiting for us on the neighbor's front porch. He was not lost; he was in the same place we left him, right at the front door.

Since that day I never lost that "Boy" again, but boyyyy have I lost other things. I lost faith. I lost my "religion." I lost hope at times, and I felt I lost my God. I left him waiting while I exited the back door and went to do other things. He was not lost, but was there all the time, in fact, he was exactly where I had left him as I languished in fun and futility, almost forgetting where he was. But when the hour was late, he was in the same place he always was. He was waiting still at the door.

But God was doing more, He was just not waiting at the door, he was knocking at the door, so that I would let him in. In the Bible in Revelation 3 (NIV), God tells us, "Here I am! I stand at the door and knock. If anyone hears my voice and opens the door, I will come in and eat with him and he with me," You have a God who is not lost and is wanting to be found so much so that he gives you a personal invitation to come and actually sit at his table just like a member of the family and dine with him.

Your verse for this journey is simple, "Seek the Lord while he may be found, call on him while he is near. (Isaiah 55:6 NIV). The shepherds found him, the Magi found him, Simeon and Anna found him, and Mary and Joseph they never lost him, and so can you. Merry Christmas Again and May God Bless You.

And the Word was made flesh, and dwelt among us, (and we beheld his glory, the as of the only begotten of the Father,) full of grace and truth.

John 1:14 (KJV)

Bonus Day
"The Name is Christian"

I did not want to close the book and finish the journey before I could challenge you to start this year, this Christmas, with a new perspective. In the Bible in Acts 11:26-29 (NIV), it tells us that in the city of Antioch, the disciples and followers of Jesus acted, looked, and talked like Christ so much so that the people around gave them the name, "Christian," which apparently meant that they were sons of Christ. It was not the disciples who called themselves that name, it was the people of Antioch who saw their behavior and knew they acted differently, therefore calling them a name that may have been derogatory to some but was a blessing to others.

I was told a story while I was living in the Middle East about Alexander the Great, that great Macedonian conqueror from Greece. He has subdued the world from Greece to India and established Greek culture throughout the world, and the story begins as this:

Alexander the Great, the commander of this vast Army was making night rounds and checking on his soldiers when he came upon a guard that was sleeping. Kicking the man to awaken him he shouted, "What is your name soldier?"

Being ashamed, not only for being asleep, but also for bearing the name, Alexander, like his commander, he reluctantly replied, "Alexander, Sir." Alexander the Great was angry and he immediately replied in the strongest admonition, "Soldier, either change your name or change your ways," for no one who was exhibiting such undisciplined behavior should ever go by the name of Alexander. You know for sure that the soldier changed his ways and was never caught sleeping again.

And I think the same can be said of those that go by the name of Christ and call themselves, "Christian." You should hold your head up high and be glad to be called after such a wonderful, powerful name, and never let it be said, that you are ashamed to be called the "sons and daughters" of our Lord. Maybe you need to change your name or change your ways.

So, let me finish by telling you a funny story to further make the point. My father and I went to the same college at the same time together, which was a real challenge for me to have your Dad in the same dorm as you and always hanging around, I mean what did the college girls think.

But one day in the chemistry class that my father was taking, after a lecture on organic formulation, the teacher who was foreign, asked if there were any questions? No one was raising their hands, and the teacher who had an accent that was hard to understand, kept asking for questions, but to my father it sounded as if he was asking if there were any, "Christians." Are there any "Christians?" My father could keep still no longer and in the middle of class he stood up and said, "Yes, I am a Christian and I am proud to be one," and went on and on, until one of the students tugged at my father's shirt and said, "Pops, he was asking if there are any questions?" Which of course made everyone laugh at my father, with the teacher still wondering what he said to bring on such a debacle.

But you see, this year, people are going to want to know if you have changed your ways, and if you are ready to voice your allegiance to Christ and be called "Christian." We do not want to ever take Christ out of Christmas, and we never want to take Christ out of you. Has the journey of 38 days ended? No, it is just beginning, come on, let's go and see what this year holds for you and me.

Joel 2:13-14 says, "Change your life, not your clothes. Come back to God, your God. And here's why: God is kind and merciful…. (The Message). It is going to be good, trust me, I know it is.

The grace of our Lord Jesus Christ be with you all. Amen.

Revelation 22:21 (KJV)

Biblical Prophecies Concerning Jesus' Birth

Jesus will be from the tribe of Judah

The scepter shall not depart from Judah, not a law-giver from between his feet until Shiloh come; and unto him shall the gathering of the people be. Genesis 49:10

Which was the son of Aminadab, which was the son of Aram, which was the son of Esrom, which was the son of Phares, which was the son of Juda. Luke 3:33

Jesus will be heir to the throne of David

Of the increase of his government and peace there shall be no end, upon the throne of David, and upon his kingdom, to order it, and to establish it with judgement and with justice from henceforth even forever. The zeal of the Lord of hosts will perform this. Isaiah 9:7

The book of the generation of Jesus Christ, the son of David, the son of Abraham. Matthew 1:1

Jesus' place of birth

But thou, Bethlehem Ephratah, though thou be little among the thousands of Judah, yet out of thee shall he come forth unto me that is to be ruler in Israel; whose goings forth have been from of old, from everlasting. Micah 5:2

Now when Jesus was born in Bethlehem of Judaea in the days of Herod the King, behold, there came wise men form the east to Jerusalem. Matthew 2:1

Jesus would be born of a virgin

Therefore the Lord himself shall give you a sign; Behold, a virgin shall conceive, and bear a son, and shall call his name Immanuel. Isaiah 7:14

To a virgin espoused to a man whose name was Joseph, of the house of David; and the virgin's name was Mary. Luke 1:27

Infants would be slaughtered after Jesus' birth

Thus saith the Lord; A voice was heard in Ramah, lamentation, and bitter weeping; Rahel weeping for her children refused to be comforted for her children, because they were not. Jeremiah 31:15

When Herod, when he saw that he was mocked of the wise men, was exceeding wroth, and sent forth, and slew all the children that were in Bethlehem, and in all the coasts thereof, about two years old and under, according to the time which he had diligently inquired of the wise men. Matthew 2:16

Jesus would be taken into Egypt

When Israel was a child, then I loved him, and called my son out of Egypt. Hosea 11:1

When he arose, he took the young child and his mother by night, and departed unto Egypt. Matthew 2:14.

Addendum

All Scripture quotations marked NIV are taken from the Holy Bible, New International Version, NIV, Copyright 1973, 1978, 1984, 2011 by Biblica, Inc. Used by permission of Zondervan. All rights reserved worldwide at www. zondervan.com. The "NIV" and the "New International Version" are trademarks registered in the United States Patent and Trademark Office by Biblica, Inc.

Scriptures marked KJV are from the King James Version of the Bible. (Public Domain).

All other portions of Scripture quoted are from The Message (msg), copyrighted by Eugene H. Peterson, 1993, 1994, 1995, 1996 and used by permission from NavPress Publishing Group and noted in the text as The Message.

Italics used in some quotes are from the author for emphasis and clarification and were not part of the original quote.

If you want more information about Christmas, please write to:

Allan Rodney Tilley

1396 Hwy 62 West

Berryville, Arkansas 72616

USA

Notes